Maths Progress

Purposeful Practice Book

Series Editors:

Dr Naomi Norman and Katherine Pate

◆ Skills practice ◆ Problem-solving practice

1

P Pearson

Published by Pearson Education Limited, 80 Strand, London, WC2R 0RL.

www.pearsonschoolsandcolleges.co.uk

Text © Pearson Education Limited 2019
Edited by Haremi Ltd.
Typeset by York Publishing Solutions Pvt. Ltd.
Cover design by Pearson Education Limited 2018
Cover illustration by Robert Samuel Hanson
Index compiled by LNS Indexing

The rights of Dr Naomi Norman, Diane Oliver, Katherine Pate and Naveen Rizvi to be identified as authors of this work has been asserted by them in accordance with the Copyright, Designs and Patents Act 1988.

First published 2019

2023
10 9 8 7

British Library Cataloguing in Publication Data
A catalogue record for this book is available from the British Library

ISBN 978 1 292 27999 2

Printed in Great Britain by Ashford Colour Press Ltd.

Note from the publisher
Pearson has robust editorial processes, including answer and fact checks, to ensure the accuracy of the content in this publication, and every effort is made to ensure this publication is free of errors. We are, however, only human, and occasionally errors do occur. Pearson is not liable for any misunderstandings that arise as a result of errors in this publication, but it is our priority to ensure that the content is accurate. If you spot an error, please do contact us at resourcescorrections@pearson.com so we can make sure it is corrected.

Contents

Maths Progress
Purposeful Practice Book 1

8 key messages from Series Editors Dr Naomi Norman and Katherine Pate

These Maths Progress Purposeful Practice books offer:

1 Lots of practice – you can never have too much!

2 Practice that develops mathematical confidence.

3 Purposeful practice questions that lead students on a path to understanding. These questions:
   - cannot be answered mechanically, by rote
   - make connections to prior knowledge
   - develop thinking skills
   - target specific concepts

4 Reflect and reason questions to:
   - make students aware of their understanding
   - show teachers what students do (or don't yet!) understand
   - encourage students to think about the underlying mathematical patterns

5 Problem-solving practice to:
   - allow students to apply their understanding to problem-solving questions and contexts
   - practise problem-solving strategies
   - lays the groundwork for GCSE exams

6 Embeds the key skills and builds confidence to succeed at KS3 by supporting the new Maths Progress (Second Edition), preparing students for their GCSEs.

7 Designed with the help of UK teachers so you can use it flexibly alongside your current resources, in class or for independent study.

8 Purposeful practice and problem-solving practice all in one book – the first of its kind.

Get to know your Purposeful Practice Book

Key points

Key points to remind students what they need to know.

⚠ Purposeful practice

The Purposeful Practice Books start with short practice questions, carefully crafted to lead students on a path to understanding the mathematics.

---

2 Number skills

2.1 Mental maths

Key points

- Partitioning splits a big number to make some easier multiplications.
- You must use the priority of operations to do calculations. Use **BIDMAS**: **B**rackets → **I**ndices (powers) → **D**ivision and **M**ultiplication → **A**ddition and **S**ubtraction
- When you have only × and ÷, or only + and −, then just work from left to right.

⚠ Purposeful practice 1

Work out

1 $6 \times 2 \times 10$	2 6×20	3 $6 \times 2 \times 10 \times 10$
4 $6 \times 20 \times 10$	5 6×200	6 $6 \times 100 \times 2$
7 $3 \times 8 \times 100$	8 3×800	9 8×300

Reflect and reason

Why are the answers to **Q3–6** the same?

Why are the answers to **Q7–9** the same?

⚠ Purposeful practice 2

Work out

1 20×7	2 4×7	3 24×7
4 $20 \times 7 + 4$	5 $20 + 4 \times 7$	6 $20 \times 7 + 4 \times 7$
7 $20 \times 7 + 40 \times 7$	8 52×6	9 $50 \times 2 \times 6$

Reflect and reason

Explain why the answers to **Q4** and **Q5** are different to the answer to **Q3**.

Explain why the answers to **Q8** and **Q9** are different.

⚠ Purposeful practice 3

Work out

1 $12 + 4 \times 2$	2 $(12 + 4) \times 2$	3 $12 \times 4 + 2$
4 $12 \times 4 \times 2$	5 $12 + 4 \times 2$	6 $12 + 4 - 2$
7 $12 + (4 - 2)$	8 $12 - 4 + 2$	9 $12 + 4 + 2$
10 $12 - 4 \times 2$	11 $12 \times 4 + 2$	12 $12 + 4 \div 2$

Reflect and reason

When did you use priority of operations? When did you work from left to right?

⊠ Problem-solving practice

1 Grace works out the answer to $3 \times 4 + 2 \times 10$.
  She writes
  $3 \times 4 + 2 \times 10 = 140$
  Grace's answer is incorrect.
  a Explain what Grace has done wrong.
  b Work out the correct answer.

2 A stamp costs 58p.
  Sian wants to buy 100 stamps.
  She has £60 to spend on stamps.
  Does Sian have enough money to buy the stamps? Explain your answer.

3 20 cars are on a ferry.
  6 of the cars have a driver but no passengers.
  9 of the cars have a driver and 1 passenger.
  5 of the cars have a driver and 2 passengers.
  Work out the total number of people in the 20 cars.
  Show your working.

4 Kelly wants to buy a magazine each month for a year.
  She can pay £4 each month or pay £42 for the year.
  Kelly pays £42 for the year.
  How much cheaper is this than paying £4 each month?
  Show your working.

5 A mobile phone network charges 8p per minute for calls and 3p per text message.
  Last week, Akram made 40 minutes of calls and sent 50 texts.
  Work out the total cost of his calls and texts last week.
  You must show your working.

6 A school orders 8 boxes of pens.
  There are 60 pens in each box.
  12 teachers take 40 pens each.
  Work out how many pens are left.
  Show your working.

7 At the start of a week, a shop has 6 full boxes of choc ices in stock.
  There are 30 choc ices in each box.
  At the end of the week there are only 17 choc ices left in the shop.
  Work out how many choc ices were sold.
  You must show your working.

8 A theatre charges £50 per ticket for a show.
  They also charge a booking fee of £2 per ticket.
  Abi, Bella and Cameron each calculate the total cost of three tickets.

  Abi writes   Bella writes   Cameron writes
  $(50 + 2) \times 3$ $3 \times 50 + 3 \times 2$ $3 \times 50 + 2$

  Who has written a correct calculation? Explain why.

9 Put sets of brackets in this calculation to give an answer of 7
  $4 + 3 \times 8 - 6 \div 2$

Reflect and reason

Thought provoking questions that encourage students to articulate a mathematical pattern, structure or relationship.

⊠ Problem-solving practice

These questions lead on from Purposeful practice, allowing students to apply the skills they have learnt in different contexts where the steps aren't obvious and they must apply different strategies.

Mixed exercises A

Mixed problem-solving practice A

1 Nisha and Zach go shopping.

  a Nisha buys the coat and the T-shirt.
     Work out the total cost.
  b Zach buys two items of clothing.
     He pays with £70 and gets £7 change.
     Which two items did Zach buy?

2 Marco writes these lists of numbers.
  Multiples of 3: 1, 3, 27, 33, 48
  Factors of 36: 3, 4, 15, 16, 18
  Square numbers: 2, 4, 6, 81, 121
  a Which numbers has Marco put in the wrong list?
  b Which of the numbers in part a belong in one of the other lists? Which list should they be in?

3 Alice earns £9 for each hour she works from Monday to Friday.
  She earns £12 for each hour she works on Saturday.
  One week, Alice worked for 5 hours on Saturday.

Mixed exercises

There are Mixed exercise pages in the book, where students can bring topics together to encourage them to make links between the mathematical concepts they have studied previously. This is to ensure that the mathematical concepts are not learnt in isolation.

How Purposeful Practice builds the skills to succeed:

△ **Purposeful practice** has been embedded in 3 different ways:

1. Variation

Carefully crafted questions that are minimally varied throughout an exercise.
As students work out the answers, they are exposed to what stays the same and what changes, from question to question. In doing so, by the end of the exercise, students deepen their understanding of the mathematical patterns, structures and relationships that underlie concepts.

2. Variation and progression

A mixture of minimally varied questions, along with small-stepped questions that get incrementally harder. These exercises are designed to both deepen understanding and move students on.

3. Progression

Questions where the skills required become incrementally harder. These small-stepped questions mean there are no uncomfortable jumps, and help to build students' confidence.

Reflect and reason

Metacognition (reflection) is a powerful tool that is used to help students become aware of their own understanding. Reasoning is a key part of the GCSE (9–1), so we've included lots of opportunities for students to show what they do (or don't yet!) understand.

⊠ **Problem-solving practice** is where the skill(s) from each sub-unit can be demonstrated and applied. These problem-solving activities will be a mixture of contextualised problems, 'working backwards' problems, and synoptic problems, ensuring that the skills practised in each sub-unit are fully embedded in new and interesting ways to build confidence.

Maths Progress Second Edition

These KS3 Purposeful Practice Books are part of *Maths Progress Second Edition*.

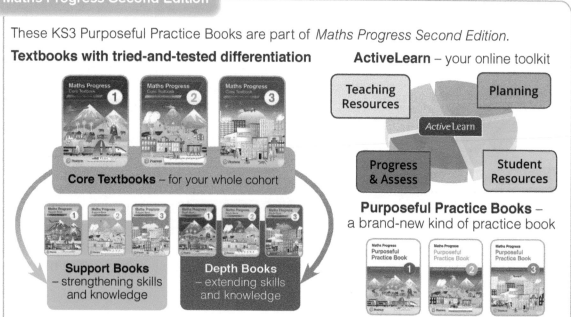

Textbooks with tried-and-tested differentiation

Core Textbooks – for your whole cohort

Support Books – strengthening skills and knowledge

Depth Books – extending skills and knowledge

ActiveLearn – your online toolkit

Teaching Resources

Planning

*Active*Learn

Progress & Assess

Student Resources

Purposeful Practice Books – a brand-new kind of practice book

For more information go to www.pearsonschools.co.uk

1 Analysing and displaying data

1.1 Mode, median and range

Key points

- Data is a set of information. Each piece of information is called a value.
- The range is the difference between the smallest and largest values. The larger the range, the more spread out the values.
- The mode is the most common value. It is also called the modal value.
- The median is the middle value when the data is written in order.

△ Purposeful practice 1

1 Work out the median for each of these sets of data.
   a 3, 3, 4, 5, 7   b 3, 3, 4, 4, 7   c 3, 3, 4, 14, 7
   d 3, 3, 4, 2, 7   e 3, 4, 4, 2, 7   f 3, 14, 4, 2, 7

2 Work out the median for each of these sets of data.
   a 3, 3, 4, 6, 7, 9   b 3, 3, 4, 6, 8, 9   c 3, 3, 4, 16, 8, 9
   d 3, 3, 4, 16, 8, 19   e 3, 3, 4, 16, 18, 19   f 3, 3, 4, 16, 14, 19

3 Work out the median for each of these sets of data.
   a 12, 12, 14, 15, 27, 29   b 12, 12, 14, 16, 27, 29 c 12, 12, 14, 30, 27, 17
   d 22, 12, 14, 30, 26, 29   e 23, 12, 14, 31, 26, 29 f 22, 23, 14, 31, 27, 29
   g 22, 22, 14, 31, 28, 29   h 22, 23, 14, 31, 28, 29, 14, 31

Reflect and reason

Are these whole numbers or decimal numbers?
- The median between two even numbers.
- The median between two odd numbers.
- The median between one odd and one even number.
Give examples from Purposeful practice 1 for each statement.

△ Purposeful practice 2

Find the range of each of these sets of data.
   1 5, 9, 16, 22   2 0, 5, 9, 16, 22   3 1, 5, 9, 16, 22
   4 2, 5, 9, 16, 22   5 3, 5, 9, 16, 22   6 4, 5, 9, 16, 22
   7 1, 5, 9, 16, 17, 22   8 1, 5, 9, 16, 22, 22   9 1, 4, 5, 9, 16, 22
  10 5, 9, 16, 22, 23   11 3, 9, 16, 22, 24   12 0, 9, 16, 22, 24, 27

Reflect and reason

When you add a value between 5 and 22 to the set 5, 9, 16, 22, the range does not change. Explain why.

△ Purposeful practice 3

1 Find the mode of each of these sets of data.

a 0, 0, 1, 2, 3   **b** 0, 1, 1, 2, 3   **c** 0, 1, 2, 2, 3

d 0, 1, 2, 3, 3   **e** 4, 7, 3, 2, 5, 2   **f** 4, 7, 3, 2, 5, 2, 2

g 4, 7, 3, 2, 5, 2, 2, 7   **h** 4, 7, 3, 2, 5, 2, 2, 7, 7, 7   **i** 4, 7, 3, 2, 5, 2, 2, 7, 7, 7, 2, 2

2 The data 5, 9, 15, 22 has a median of 12.
Work out the new median when

a 0 is added (to give 0, 5, 9, 15, 22)   **b** 1 is added

c 7 is added   **d** 11 is added   **e** 12 is added

f 17 is added   **g** 20 is added   **h** 25 is added

Reflect and reason

When you add a value higher than the original median, is the new median higher or lower than the original median?

⊠ Problem-solving practice

1 One number in each list is missing.
The mode of each list is 7.
What is the missing number in each case?

a 3, ☐, 7   **b** 2, 3, ☐, 7, 9   **c** 5, 5, 6, ☐, 7, 7

2 One number in each list is missing.
The median of each list is 4.
What is the missing number in each case?

a 1, ☐, 5   **b** 0, 3, ☐, 6, 8   **c** 2, 2, 3, ☐, 7, 10

3 11, 13, 14, 17, 22, 10, 18
Taylor says, 'The median of these numbers is 17.'
Taylor is incorrect. Explain why.

4 These are the shoe sizes of some students.
4, 5, 6, 5, 5, 7, 8, 10, 4, 3

a What is the mode of the shoe sizes?

b What is the range of the shoe sizes?

c A new student with shoe size 6 joins the class.
Does this change the range of the shoe sizes of the children in the class?
Explain your answer.

d Another new student joins the class. The range increases by 1.
Write down all the possible shoe sizes that the new student could have.

5 4, 10, 6, ☐
One number is missing from this list.
The range is 7.
What could the missing number be?

6 There are four numbers: ☐, ☐, ☐, ☐
The mode of the four numbers is 9 and the median is 8.
The smallest value is 2.
Write the four numbers in order from smallest to largest.

Key points

- You can record data in a tally chart. Use a tally mark | for each value. Group tally marks in fives. The frequency of a value is the number of times it occurs.
- A bar chart uses bars of equal width to show data.
- A bar-line chart is like a bar chart but uses lines instead of bars.
- A pictogram uses pictures to show data. The key explains the pictures.

Purposeful practice 1

The colours of 33 cats in a rescue centre are recorded, using letters to represent each colour: G (Ginger), B (Black), T (Tabby) and W (White).

B, G, B, G, T, B, B, T, T, W, T, B, G, B, T, B, B, W, B, T, B, B, T, B, W, G, T, B, B, T, G, T, B

1   Make a tally chart for the data. Include the columns 'colour', 'tally' and 'frequency'.

2   Copy and complete this pictogram for the data.

Colours of cats

Ginger
Black
Tabby
White

Key: ⊗ represents 5 cats

3   Copy and complete this bar chart for the data.

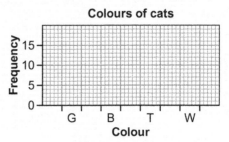

Colours of cats

4   Draw a bar-line chart for the data.
Use axes like the ones in **Q3**.

Reflect and reason

What is the same and what is different about the charts and tables you drew in **Q1–4**?

Purposeful practice 2

Find the mode and, where possible, the range of each set of data.

1   **Numbers of red sweets in various packets**

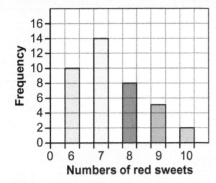

2 Flavours of sweets in a packet

Strawberry	🍬 🍬 🍬 🍬
Lime	🍬 🍬 🍬
Lemon	🍬 🍬 🍬
Chocolate	🍬 🍬

Key: 🍬 represents 2 sweets

Reflect and reason

What type of data does not have a range? Can this type of data have a mode? Use examples from this page to explain.

⊠ Problem-solving practice

1 Students in a class are asked to choose their favourite sport.
The table and the bar chart show information about the results.

Sport	Frequency
football	12
netball	9
swimming	
tennis	

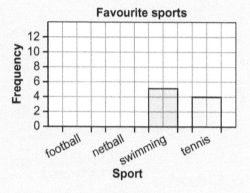
Favourite sports

a Copy the table and use the bar chart to complete the table.

b Copy the bar chart and use the table to complete the bar chart.

2 The pictogram shows the number of mobile phones sold in a shop on Monday, Tuesday and Wednesday.
a How many phones were sold on Monday?
b More mobile phones were sold on Tuesday than on Wednesday. How many more?
On Thursday, 2 mobile phones were sold.
On Friday, 24 mobile phones were sold.
c Copy the pictogram and complete it for Thursday and Friday.
d Which day is the mode?

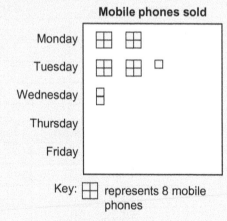
Mobile phones sold

Key: ⊞ represents 8 mobile phones

3 Yuri saves coins of different values.
The line graph gives information about the numbers of coins he saves.
a What is the modal coin value?
b Yuri had no coins of one value. What value of coin is this?
c Yuri has more 50p coins than £1 coins. How many more?
d Work out his total number of coins.

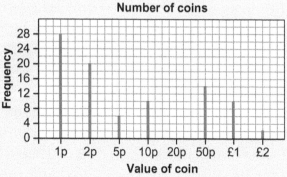
Number of coins

Key points

- Data is sometimes organised into groups or classes, such as 1–5, 6–10, 11–15, ...
- For data that comes from measuring, such as height, there are no gaps between the bars of a bar chart.

△ Purposeful practice 1

Jim draws a tally chart to record the number of 'likes' on social media posts.

1 Jim wants to record 30, 20 and 40 'likes'. Explain why he cannot record these in his tally chart.

Number of likes	Tally	Frequency
0–10		
10–20		
20–30		
30–40		
40–50		

2 Redraw Jim's tally chart so that he can record all results up to 50. Put these results in your tally chart: 30, 20, 40, 15, 19, 41, 50, 39, 1

Reflect and reason

Daisy wants to record her test marks in groups like this: 0–5, 5–10, 10–15, 15–20, ... Explain why this will not work. Suggest how Daisy could group her results.

△ Purposeful practice 2

Copy and complete the grouped bar chart for each set of data.

1

Number of birds	Frequency
0–5	5
6–10	8
11–15	2
16–20	3

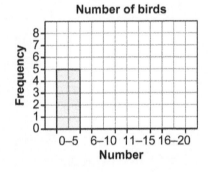

2

Weight of parcels (kg)	Frequency
0–5	5
6–10	8
11–15	2
16–20	3

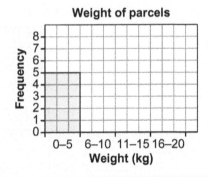

Reflect and reason

Class 7 draws bar charts for these sets of data.

A Number of leaves   **B** Lengths of leaves   **C** Weights of animals
D Speeds of animals   **E** Numbers of animals

Which bar charts should have gaps between the bars? Explain.

⊠ Problem-solving practice

1 The data shows the number of books people own.

41, 44, 50, 55, 59, 60, 61, 67, 68, 70, 75, 80, 90

The data is put into a grouped frequency table using groups of 10.

Which frequency table is correct? Give reasons for your answer.

A

Number of books	Frequency
41–50	
51–60	
61–70	
71–80	
81–90	

B

Number of books	Frequency
40–50	
50–60	
60–70	
80–90	
80–90	

C

Number of books	Frequency
40–49	
50–59	
60–69	
70–79	
80–90	
90+	

2 Sam measures the height of the children in his class.
The table shows his results.
Draw a bar chart for Sam's results.

Height (cm)	Frequency
141–145	2
146–150	6
151–155	8
156–160	11
161–165	3

3 The table and the bar chart show information about
the age of teachers working at a school.

Age (in years)	Frequency
21–30	7
31–40	

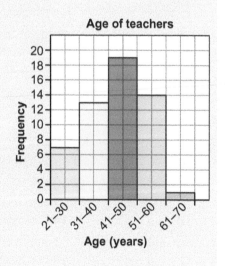

Age of teachers

a Copy the table and use the bar chart to
complete the table.

b How many teachers are aged 41 or over?

Key point

- The mean of a set of values is the total of the set of values divided by the number of values.

△ Purposeful practice 1

1 What number should you divide by to calculate the mean for each set of data?
   a 3, 3, 4, 5   b 3, 3, 4, 4, 7   c 3, 3, 4, 14, 7
   d 3, 3, 4, 0, 7   e 3, 4, 4, 0, 7, 0   f 3, 4, 4, 0, 7, 0, 10

2 The data 1, 2, 2, 3 has mean 2.
   Work out the new mean when
   a 0 is added (to give 0, 1, 2, 2, 3)   b 1 is added
   c 2 is added   d 3 is added   e 4 is added

3 The mean of this data is 5.
   3.7, 4.3, 5.5, 4.5, 6, 6
   a Would the mean increase or decrease when you remove the largest value from the data?
   b Would the mean increase or decrease when you remove the smallest value from the data?

4 a Find the mean of this set of data: 0, 4, 7, 13, 16
   b In parts i to vi, one extra value is added to the data set, as shown in red.
     Does the mean increase, decrease or stay the same in each case?
       i 0, 0, 4, 7, 13, 16   ii 0, 4, 7, 10, 13, 16   iii 0, 4, 5, 7, 13, 16
      iv 0, 4, 7, 8, 13, 16   v 0, 4, 7, 9, 13, 16   vi 0, 4, 7, 13, 16, 17

Reflect and reason

Does adding another value to a set of data always change the mean?
Explain how the mean changes when you add values less than or greater than the mean.

△ Purposeful practice 2

1 Find the mean when there are
   a 10 values that add up to 30   b 5 values that add up to 30
   c 2 values that add up to 30   d 6 values that add up to 30
   e 3 values that add up to 30   f 20 values that add up to 30
   g 30 values that add up to 30   h 60 values that add up to 30

2 Find the number of values in the data set when
   a the mean is 10 and the total of values is 40
   b the mean is 5 and the total of values is 40
   c the mean is 8 and the total of values is 40
   d the mean is 20 and the total of values is 40
   e the mean is 2 and the total of values is 40
   f the mean is 1 and the total of values is 40
   g the mean is 0.5 and the total of values is 40

3 Find the total of the values in the data set when

    a 5 values have mean = 10   **b** 4 values have mean = 10

    c 2 values have mean = 10   **d** 7 values have mean = 10

    e 17 values have mean = 10   **f** 25 values have mean = 10

    g 40 values have mean = 10

Reflect and reason

20 people raise money for charity. The mean amount raised is £5.

Who has correctly worked out the total amount raised? Explain your answer.

Sam	Alex	Jo
20 × £5 = £100	£20 ÷ 5 = £4	£5 ÷ 20 = £0.25

⊠ Problem-solving practice

1 Here are three lists of numbers.

  One number in each list is missing and the mean of each list is 6.

  What is the missing number in each case?

    a 3, ☐

    b 3, ☐, 9

    c 3, ☐, 9, 9

2 Here is a list of 10 numbers.

  2, 0, 1, 3, 4, 2, 0, 1, 2, 1

    a Work out the mean of the 10 numbers.

  The 11th number is 3.

    b Will the mean for all 11 numbers be greater than or less than the mean number of the first 10 numbers? Explain your answer.

3 Here are five number cards.

7	8	11		15

  One of the cards is turned over so you cannot see the number on it.

  The mean of the five numbers is 10.

  Work out the number you cannot see.

4 Six children sit a test.

  The scores for five of the children are shown.

  12, 15, 20, 22, 23

  The mean for the six children is 17.

  Work out the test score for the sixth child.

5 Abi saves her photos on a memory card.

  The memory card has 16 000 megabytes of storage space.

  Each photo uses an average of 4.8 megabytes of storage.

  Abi has saved 900 photos on the memory card.

  Work out how much more storage space is left on the memory card.

Key points

- A dual bar chart compares two sets of data.
- A compound bar chart combines different sets of data in one bar.

⚠ Purposeful practice 1

These graphs show the numbers of lunch and dinner customers at a cafe each day.

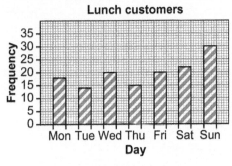
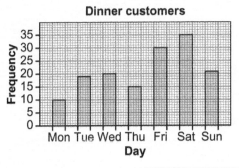

1 Copy and complete the dual bar chart shown to combine the two graphs. Give your graph a key and a title.

2 Which days had more lunch customers than dinner customers?

3 Which days had more dinner customers than lunch customers?

4 Which days had the same number of lunch and dinner customers?

5 Which day had the most customers in total?

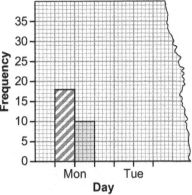

Reflect and reason

Was it easier to answer **Q2–5** using your dual bar chart or the separate bar charts? Give reasons for your answer.

⚠ Purposeful practice 2

This compound bar chart shows the numbers of dogs and cats a vet sees each day.

1 Write down the number of cats and the number of dogs for each day.

2 Which days did the vet see an equal number of dogs and cats?

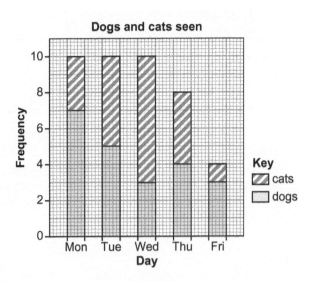

3 On Saturday the vet saw 3 dogs, 1 cat and 4 rabbits.
Draw a compound bar to show this.

Reflect and reason

Lucy says, 'The vet saw 7 dogs and 10 cats on Monday.' What mistake has she made?

⊠ Problem-solving practice

1 The dual bar chart shows information about the number of text messages Emily and Toby sent on each day in a week.
Emily says, 'I sent twice as many text messages as Toby.'
Is Emily correct? Explain how you know.

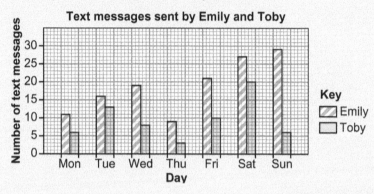

2 Daria asks four football fans how many matches they attended home and away during a season. The compound bar chart shows Daria results.
Copy the table and use the compound bar chart to complete the table for Daria's results.

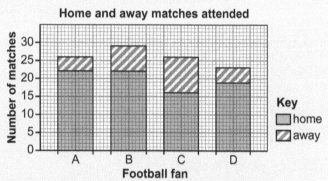

	Fan A	Fan B	Fan C	Fan D
Number of matches at home				
Number of matches away				

3 The table shows information about the number of students in Year 7 and Year 8 who play different instruments.

	Instrument				
	clarinet	violin	piano	saxophone	drums
Year 7	25	20	10	15	10
Year 8	12	18	15	15	20

Draw a suitable diagram to show this information.

2 Number skills

Key points

- Partitioning splits a big number to make some easier multiplications.
- You must use the priority of operations to do calculations. Use **BIDMAS**:
  Brackets → **I**ndices (powers) → **D**ivision and **M**ultiplication → **A**ddition and **S**ubtraction
- When you have only × and ÷, or only + and −, then just work from left to right.

△ Purposeful practice 1

Work out

1 $6 \times 2 \times 10$	**2** 6×20	**3** $6 \times 2 \times 10 \times 10$
4 $6 \times 20 \times 10$	**5** 6×200	**6** $6 \times 100 \times 2$
7 $3 \times 8 \times 100$	**8** 3×800	**9** 8×300

Reflect and reason

Why are the answers to **Q3–6** the same?

Why are the answers to **Q7–9** the same?

△ Purposeful practice 2

Work out

1 20×7	**2** 4×7	**3** 24×7
4 $20 \times 7 + 4$	**5** $20 + 4 \times 7$	**6** $20 \times 7 + 4 \times 7$
7 $20 \times 7 + 40 \times 7$	**8** 52×6	**9** $50 \times 2 \times 6$

Reflect and reason

Explain why the answers to **Q4** and **Q5** are different to the answer to **Q3**.

Explain why the answers to **Q8** and **Q9** are different.

△ Purposeful practice 3

Work out

1 $12 + 4 \times 2$	**2** $(12 + 4) \times 2$	**3** $12 \times 4 + 2$
4 $12 \times 4 \times 2$	**5** $12 \div 4 \times 2$	**6** $12 \div 4 - 2$
7 $12 \div (4 - 2)$	**8** $12 - 4 \div 2$	**9** $12 \div 4 + 2$
10 $12 - 4 \times 2$	**11** $12 \times 4 \div 2$	**12** $12 \div 4 \div 2$

Reflect and reason

When did you use priority of operations? When did you work from left to right?

1 Grace works out the answer to $3 \times 4 + 2 \times 10$.
She writes

$3 \times 4 + 2 \times 10 = 140$

Grace's answer is incorrect.
a Explain what Grace has done wrong.
b Work out the correct answer.

2 A stamp costs 58p.
Sian wants to buy 100 stamps.
She has £60 to spend on stamps.
Does Sian have enough money to buy the stamps? Explain your answer.

3 20 cars are on a ferry.
6 of the cars have a driver but no passengers.
9 of the cars have a driver and 1 passenger.
5 of the cars have a driver and 2 passengers.
Work out the total number of people in the 20 cars.
Show your working.

4 Kelly wants to buy a magazine each month for a year.
She can pay £4 each month or pay £42 for the year.
Kelly pays £42 for the year.
How much cheaper is this than paying £4 each month?
Show your working.

5 A mobile phone network charges 8p per minute for calls and 3p per text message.
Last week, Akram made 40 minutes of calls and sent 50 texts.
Work out the total cost of his calls and texts last week.
You must show your working.

6 A school orders 8 boxes of pens.
There are 60 pens in each box.
12 teachers take 40 pens each.
Work out how many pens are left.
Show your working.

7 At the start of a week, a shop has 6 full boxes of choc ices in stock.
There are 30 choc ices in each box.
At the end of the week there are only 17 choc ices left in the shop.
Work out how many choc ices were sold.
You must show your working.

8 A theatre charges £50 per ticket for a show.
They also charge a booking fee of £2 per ticket.
Abi, Bella and Cameron each calculate the total cost of three tickets.

Abi writes	Bella writes	Cameron writes
$(50 + 2) \times 3$	$3 \times 50 + 3 \times 2$	$3 \times 50 + 2$

Who has written a correct calculation? Explain why.

9 Put sets of brackets in this calculation to give an answer of 7
$4 + 3 \times 8 - 6 \div 2$

Key points

- Addition and subtraction are inverse operations.
- For rounding, if a digit is less than 5, round down. If it's 5 or more, round up.
  To round to the nearest 10, look at the digit in the units column.
  To round to the nearest 100, look at the digit in the tens column.
  To round to the nearest 1000, look at the digit in the hundreds column.

△ Purposeful practice 1

1 Work out

a 461 + 132	**b** 462 + 132	**c** 461 + 133
d 461 + 142	**e** 461 + 152	**f** 471 + 152
g 471 + 252	**h** 471 + 352	**i** 571 + 352

2 Work out

a 756 − 541	**b** 757 − 541	**c** 757 − 542
d 757 − 551	**e** 757 − 561	**f** 767 − 561
g 767 − 661	**h** 767 − 761	**i** 867 − 771

Reflect and reason

724 + 265 = 989

How can you use this addition calculation to work out

a 724 + 275   **b** 824 + 265?

△ Purposeful practice 2

Copy and complete each calculation.

1 a 384 + 213 = ☐   **b** 597 − ☐ = 213   **c** 597 − ☐ = 384
2 a 1274 + 655 = ☐   **b** 1929 − ☐ = 1274   **c** 1929 − ☐ = 655
3 a 936 − 713 = ☐   **b** 223 + ☐ = 936   **c** 936 − ☐ = 223

Reflect and reason

Write two related calculations for

a 867 + 429   **b** 902 − 471

△ Purposeful practice 3

		a 10	**b** 100		
1	Round 98 to the nearest	**a** 10	**b** 100		
2	Round 984 to the nearest	**a** 10	**b** 100	**c** 1000	
3	Round 9984 to the nearest	**a** 10	**b** 100	**c** 1000	**d** 10 000
4	Round 39 984 to the nearest	**a** 10	**b** 100	**c** 1000	**d** 10 000

Reflect and reason

Why did **Q3** parts **b**, **c** and **d** give the same answer?

1 Farrah is asked to work out 542 + 173.
Farrah writes

```
    5 4 2
  + 1 7 3
    6 1 5
      1
```

    a Use rounding to the nearest 100 to check Farrah's calculation.
    b What mistake has Farrah made?
    c Work out the correct answer.

2 Alan is asked to write three calculations related to 357 + 684 = 1041
Alan writes

1041 − 684 = 357
684 − 357 = 1041
1041 − 357 = 684

One of Alan's calculations is incorrect.
Which calculation is incorrect?
Explain what Alan has done wrong.

3 Two trains arrive at a station.
Train A has 132 passengers.
Train B has 219 passengers.

    a How many passengers are there altogether?
       You must show your working.
    b Train B has more passengers than train A.
       How many more?
       You must show your working.

4 Here is an addition pyramid.

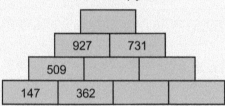

The number in any brick is the sum of the numbers in the two bricks below.
For example, 147 + 362 = 509
Copy and complete the addition pyramid.

5 Copy each calculation and work out the missing digits.

    a
```
    4 □ 5
  + □ 3 6
    7 1 □
```

    b
```
    8 5 □
  − 3 □ 7
    □ 2 3
```

Key point

- In the column method, you write the numbers in the calculation in their place value columns.

$$\begin{array}{r} 2\ 4\ 2 \\ \times \qquad 3 \\ \hline \end{array}$$

△ Purposeful practice 1

Use the column method or otherwise to work out each multiplication.

1 313×3 **2** 314×3 **3** 315×3

4 342×4 **5** 343×4 **6** 344×4

7 619×5 **8** 620×5 **9** 621×5

Reflect and reason

Adrian worked out the answer to **Q2** by adding 3 to his answer to **Q1**. Is he correct? Explain why.

How can you use your answer to **Q7** to work out the answers to **Q8** and **Q9**?

△ Purposeful practice 2

Work out

1 152×7 **2** 151×7 **3** 150×7

4 481×6 **5** 480×6 **6** 479×6

7 479×5 **8** 479×4 **9** 479×7

Reflect and reason

Lisa worked out the answer to **Q2** by subtracting 7 from her answer to **Q1**. Is she correct? Explain why.

Look carefully at **Q6**, **Q7** and **Q8**. How can you use your answer to **Q6** to work out the answers to **Q7** and **Q8**?

△ Purposeful practice 3

Work out each multiplication.

1 **a**
$$\begin{array}{r} 6\ 2 \\ \times \qquad 8 \\ \hline \end{array}$$
b
$$\begin{array}{r} 6\ 2 \\ \times\ 8\ 0 \\ \hline \end{array}$$
c
$$\begin{array}{r} 6\ 2 \\ \times\ 8\ 8 \\ \hline \end{array}$$
d
$$\begin{array}{r} 6\ 2 \\ \times\ 1\ 8 \\ \hline \end{array}$$

e
$$\begin{array}{r} 6\ 2 \\ \times\ 8\ 1 \\ \hline \end{array}$$
f
$$\begin{array}{r} 2\ 6 \\ \times\ 1\ 8 \\ \hline \end{array}$$
g
$$\begin{array}{r} 2\ 6 \\ \times\ 8\ 1 \\ \hline \end{array}$$

2 a 318×4 **b** 318×14 **c** 318×41
d 2318×5 **e** 2318×15 **f** 2318×51

Reflect and reason

Rohil works out this multiplication.
What mistake has he made?
What is the correct answer?

$$
\begin{array}{r}
7\ 2 \\
\times\ 1\ 9 \\
\hline
6\ 4^{1}\ 8 \\
7\ 2 \\
\hline
7\ 2\ 0 \\
\scriptstyle 1
\end{array}
$$

⊠ Problem-solving practice

1 A theme park charges £42 per person.
A group of 18 people visit the theme park.
Work out the total cost of their visit.
You must show your working.

2 Vina goes to watch 16 football matches in a year.
Each match ticket costs £28.
Vina says, 'I spend £448 a year on football matches.'
Is Vina correct? Use a calculation to explain why.

3 Jordan correctly works out $457 \times 6 = 2742$
Jordan then says, 'This means that $458 \times 6 = 2743$ because 458 is one more than 457 so just add 1 to the answer.'
  a Explain why Jordan is incorrect.
  b Write the correct answer to 458×6

4 Remi hires 14 coaches to take 748 people to a netball match.
Each coach can take 52 people.
Has Remi hired enough coaches?
You must show your working.

5 Duncan sees these two adverts for jobs.

Job A
24 hours a week
£15 per hour.

Job B
28 hours a week
£13 per hour.

Which job pays more per week?
You must show your working.

6 At the start of a week, a shop has 27 full boxes of sweets in stock.
There are 36 packets of sweets in each box.
By the end of the week there are 25 packets of sweets left in the shop.
Work out how may packets of sweets the shop sold.
You must show your working.

7 Copy and complete this multiplication:

$$
\begin{array}{r}
4\ 3\ 7 \\
\times\ \ \ \square \\
\hline
\square\ 4\ 9\ 6 \\
\end{array}
$$

Key points

- Multiplication and division are inverse operations.
- Long division is a written method to divide numbers with two or more digits. It breaks down the calculation into smaller steps than short division.

△ Purposeful practice 1

Copy and complete each calculation.

1 a $3\overline{)99}$ **b** $3 \times \square = 99$ **c** $33 \times \square = 99$

2 a $8\overline{)216}$ **b** $8 \times \square = 216$ **c** $27 \times \square = 216$

3 a $7\overline{)3612}$ **b** $7 \times \square = 3612$ **c** $516 \times \square = 3612$

Reflect and reason

Write two calculations for

a $6\overline{)2754}$ **b** 9×37

△ Purposeful practice 2

1 Use long division to work out these calculations. Parts **a** and **d** have been started for you.

a $15\overline{)465}$
  3
  45
  $\overline{15}$

b $15\overline{)495}$

c $15\overline{)4950}$

d $15\overline{)4095}$
  2
  30

e $21\overline{)588}$

f $21\overline{)5859}$

g $21\overline{)5901}$

h $888 \div 37$

i $999 \div 37$

2 Work out these divisions with remainders.

a $11\overline{)177}$ **b** $13\overline{)300}$ **c** $16\overline{)562}$

d $31\overline{)375}$ **e** $24\overline{)605}$ **f** $42\overline{)1180}$

g $53\overline{)1168}$ **h** $1027 \div 35$ **i** $1069 \div 29$

Reflect and reason

Sally works out $354 \div 18$

What mistake has Sally made?

What is the correct answer?

$18\overline{)3\overset{4}{5}4}$
  12
  18
  $\overline{36}$ ← 2×18

1 Harriet is asked to write three calculations related to $136 \times 17 = 2312$
   $2312 \div 136 = 17$
   $136 \div 17 = 2312$
   $2312 \div 17 = 136$
   One of Harriet's calculations is incorrect.
   Which calculation is incorrect?
   Explain what Harriet has done wrong.

2 Tariq is asked to work out $675 \div 21$ using long division.
   Tariq writes

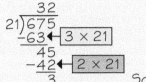

   So $675 \div 21 = 3$ remainder 32

   Tariq is incorrect. What mistake has he made?

3 Caitlin pays the same amount each month into a savings account.
   She has been saving for 19 months.
   She now has £1235 in the account.
   Work out how much money Caitlin has saved each month.
   You must show your working.

4 Helen has 500 eggs.
   She wants to put all the eggs into boxes.
   She can put 15 eggs into each box.
   How many full boxes will Helen have?
   You must show your working.

5 Claudia is buying a car that costs £14 500.
   She pays £1900 at the start.
   She pays the rest in equal payments over 24 months.
   Work out how much Claudia pays each month.
   You must show your working.

6 Arif is going to make some cupcakes.
   He needs 22 grams of flour for each cupcake.
   Arif wants to make 15 cupcakes.
   He has 325 grams of flour.
   Does Arif have enough flour for the cupcakes?
   You must show how you got your answer.

7 **a** The digits 2, 3, 4 and 5 are arranged as a division calculation.
       $2\overline{)345}$
       Work out the answer.

   b Arrange the digits 3, 4, 5 and 6 as a division calculation.
       Write one digit in each box.

       i What is the smallest possible answer?
       ii What is the largest possible answer?

Key points

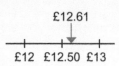

- To round an amount to the nearest pound, look at the pence.
  £12.61 rounds up to £13
- To round an amount to the nearest penny, look at the number after the pence.
  For 3.426 it is 6, so round up to £3.43
  For 7.22349 it is 3, so round down to £7.22
- Time can be written as a decimal number of hours, for example 0.25 hours is $\frac{1}{4}$ of an hour or 15 minutes (not 25 minutes), and 1.25 hours = 1 hour 15 minutes.

△ Purposeful practice 1

1 Round each amount to the nearest pound.

a £7.49	b £7.50	c £7.51	d £7.15
e £74.90	f £75.50	g £75.09	h £107.07

2 Each calculator display shows an amount of money. Round it to the nearest penny.

a 12.404	b 12.409	c 12.405	d 12.483
e 12.4832	f 12.4839	g 102.0917	h 102.0997

Reflect and reason

How do you know when to round up or down when working with money?

What was the same and what was different when you rounded the calculator money answers to the nearest penny in **Q2** parts **g** and **h**?

△ Purposeful practice 2

Round each amount to the nearest

a pound   b penny

1 1.992	2 1.997	3 2.993
4 2.998	5 99.991	6 99.999

Reflect and reason

Why do **Q1a**, **Q2a** and **Q2b** have answers that are the same amounts of money?

△ Purposeful practice 3

1 Copy the table and fill in the missing values.

Time (decimal of an hour)	0	0.2	0.5		1
Time (fraction of an hour)	0			$\frac{3}{4}$	1
Time (minutes)	0		30		

2 Match the times to the decimals.

1 hour 15 minutes	1 hour 45 minutes	4.75	1.25
4 hours 45 minutes	25 hours 45 minutes	15.5	25.5
15 hours 30 minutes	25 hours 15 minutes	25.25	15.25
25 hours 30 minutes	15 hours 15 minutes	1.75	25.75

3 Write these as decimals.

   a $2\frac{1}{4}$ hours   **b** $2\frac{3}{4}$ hours   **c** $4\frac{1}{2}$ hours   **d** $32\frac{1}{4}$ hours   **e** $42\frac{1}{2}$ hours

Reflect and reason

Kamal uses his calculator to work out the answer to a time calculation in hours.
His calculator display shows 6.25

He says. 'The answer is 6 hours 25 minutes.'
Why is this wrong? What is the correct answer?

⊠ Problem-solving practice

1 Pete uses his calculator to work out the answer to a money calculation in pounds.
His calculator display shows 42.3681

Pete says, 'This rounds to £42.36 because the last digit is 1 so I need to round down.'
   a Explain why Pete is wrong.   **b** What is 42.3681 rounded to the nearest penny?

2 Erin uses her calculator to work out the answer to a time calculation in hours and
minutes. Her calculator display shows the answer 3.5

Erin says, 'The answer is 3 hours and 5 minutes.'
   a Explain why Erin is wrong.   **b** What is the correct answer in hours and minutes?

3 Finn uses his calculator to work out the answer to a time calculation.
For his calculation, Finn needs to type in $1\frac{3}{4}$ hours as a decimal.
Finn says, '$1\frac{3}{4}$ is 1 hour and 45 minutes so I need to put 1.45 into my calculator.'
   a Explain why Finn is wrong.
   b What is the correct number that Finn should put in his calculator?

4 Raj buys one of each item shown to build a
computer.
Round the cost of each item to the nearest pound
to estimate the total cost of all five items. You must
show your working.

| Printer £165.75 | Monitor £135.55 | Tower £347.49 |
| Keyboard £37.40 | Mouse £15.80 | |

5 As soon as Callum gets home he spends $1\frac{1}{4}$ hours on his homework.
He then takes 30 minutes to have his dinner.
Then he spends 1.5 hours watching TV.
   a Work out how long Callum has spent at home so far in hours and minutes.
   b Write your answer to part **a** in hours as a decimal.

Key points

- You can show positive and negative numbers on a number line.

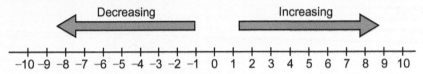

- The symbol > means 'is greater than'.
  The symbol < means 'is less than'.

△ Purposeful practice 1

1 Work out the missing numbers on each number line.

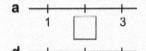

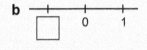

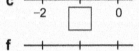

2 Copy and complete each calculation. Fill in the gap with < or >

a 5 ☐ 4	**b** 5 ☐ −4	**c** −5 ☐ 4	**d** −5 ☐ −4
e −4 ☐ −5	**f** 0 ☐ −5	**g** 20 ☐ −10	**h** −20 ☐ 10
i −20 ☐ 0	**j** 0 ☐ −10	**k** −10 ☐ −20	**l** −100 ☐ −20

Reflect and reason

Felix says, '16 is greater than 15, so −16 is greater than −15.'

Is he correct? Explain your answer.

△ Purposeful practice 2

Work out each calculation.

1
a 4 − 2	**b** 3 − 2	**c** 2 − 2	**d** 1 − 2
e 0 − 2	**f** −1 − 2	**g** −2 − 2	**h** −3 − 2
i −3 − 3	**j** −3 − 4	**k** −3 − 5	**l** −4 − 5

2
a −5 + 3	**b** −4 + 3	**c** −3 + 3	**d** −2 + 3
e −1 + 3	**f** 0 + 3	**g** −5 + 4	**h** −5 + 5
i −12 + 8	**j** −12 + 9	**k** −12 − 8	**l** −12 − 9

3 Which calculations give an answer of

a 10	**b** −10	**c** neither 10 nor −10?	
A −6 − 4	B −6 + 14	C −6 + 16	D −6 + 4
E −4 + 6	F −4 + 14	G −8 + 2	H −8 − 2
I −8 + 12	J −8 + 18	K −2 + 12	L −2 − 12

4 For each calculation, write if it gives a positive or negative answer.
(You do not need to work out the exact answer.)

   a $28 - 30$ **b** $-28 + 30$ **c** $-28 - 30$

   d $-30 - 48$ **e** $30 - 48$ **f** $-38 + 48$

   g $308 - 314$ **h** $-314 + 308$ **i** $-314 - 308$

Reflect and reason

Antony knows that $46 + 54 = 100$. He writes

$-46 + 54 = 100$ and $46 - 54 = -100$

Is he correct? If not, write the correct answers.

⊠ Problem-solving practice

1 Write these numbers in order of size. Start with the smallest number.

   5   -6 1 -3 -10

2 Gavin and Jason work out the answer to $-5 + 3$.

   Gavin writes   Jason writes

   $-5 + 3 = 8$ $-5 + 3 = 2$

   They have both written the wrong answer.

   a Explain what they have each done wrong.   **b** Work out the correct answer.

3 **a** At 7 am, the temperature was $-5\,°C$.
     By 3 pm, the temperature had risen by $9\,°C$.
     Write the temperature at 3 pm.

   b At 9 pm, the temperature was $-2\,°C$.
     By midnight, the temperature had gone down by $6\,°C$.
     Write the temperature at midnight.

4 The table shows the temperatures in Toronto for five days during one week.

Day	Maximum temperature	Minimum temperature
Monday	$-1\,°C$	$-6\,°C$
Tuesday	$-6\,°C$	$-12\,°C$
Wednesday	$2\,°C$	$-12\,°C$
Thursday	$6\,°C$	$-9\,°C$
Friday	$-8\,°C$	$-14\,°C$

   a Which day had the highest maximum temperature?

   b What is the lowest minimum temperature?

   c Which day had the greatest difference between the maximum temperature and the minimum temperature?

5 **a** Use the numbers -10, 2, 4 and 8 to complete this calculation.

     ☐ $-$ ☐ $=$ ☐ $+$ ☐

   b Can you find more than one way of answering part **a**?

6 Joe is thinking of two numbers. One number is positive and the other is negative.
The total of his two numbers is -5. What two numbers might Joe be thinking of?

Key points

- A factor is a whole number that will divide exactly into another number.
- A multiple of a number is in that number's multiplication table.
- The highest common factor (HCF) of two numbers is the largest number that is a factor of both numbers.
- The lowest common multiple (LCM) of two numbers is the smallest number that is a multiple of both numbers.

△ Purposeful practice 1

1 Write all the factors of each number.

 a 2 **b** 4 **c** 8 **d** 16 **e** 32

 f 64 **g** 7 **h** 14 **i** 28 **j** 56

2 Write the first six multiples of each number.

 a 5 **b** 15 **c** 25 **d** 50 **e** 75 **f** 150

Reflect and reason

Crista lists all the factors of 15

3, 5

Is her list correct? If not, write the correct list.

Crista now lists the first six multiples of 30

1, 2, 3, 5, 6, 10

What mistake has Crista made? Write the correct list.

△ Purposeful practice 2

Work out the highest common factor (HCF) of these pairs of numbers.

1 4 and 14   **2** 4 and 28   **3** 4 and 32

4 8 and 20   **5** 8 and 25   **6** 8 and 40

7 8 and 50   **8** 8 and 55   **9** 8 and 80

Reflect and reason

When is the HCF one of the numbers in the pair?
Is it the smaller or larger number in the pair?

△ Purposeful practice 3

Work out the lowest common multiple (LCM) of each pair of numbers.

1 5 and 15   **2** 5 and 25   **3** 5 and 11

4 5 and 12   **5** 5 and 50   **6** 15 and 25

7 30 and 50   **8** 25 and 75   **9** 75 and 100

> **Reflect and reason**
> When is the LCM one of the numbers in the pair?
> Is it the smaller or larger number in the pair?

⊠ Problem-solving practice

1 Abdul is asked to list all the factors of 12.
He writes
1, 2, 3, 4, 5, 6
Write two mistakes that Abdul has made.

2 Chris is asked to list the first six multiples of 7.
Chris writes
14, 21, 28, 35, 42, 49
What mistake has Chris made?

3 Here is a list of numbers.
1, 2, 4, 5, 7, 11, 13, 14, 15, 17
From the list, write two factors of 60 that add together to make 20.

4 Siu writes the factors of 72 that are single digits and adds them together.
Write the total that Siu gets.

5 Louis lists the factors of 60.
He chooses two of the factors from his list and adds them together.
The total of the two factors Louis chooses is 10.
Write these two factors.

6 Write a number that is
a a multiple of 6 and a factor of 60
b a factor of both 30 and 48
c a multiple of both 4 and 7

7 Sara writes
The multiples of 3 are 3, 6, 9, 12, 15, 18, ...
So, all multiples for any number are in the pattern odd, even, odd, even, and so on.
Write the multiples of another number to show that Sara is wrong.

8 Write two numbers that have a highest common factor of 12.

9 Jake lists the common factors of 28 and 48.
He chooses two of the numbers from his list.
The total of the two numbers is 6.
What are the two numbers?

10 Jacinta is asked to work out the lowest common multiple of 20 and 30.
She says, 'The answer is 10.'
a Explain what Jacinta has done wrong.
b Work out the correct answer.

11 **a** Write two numbers that have a highest common factor of 40.
b Write two numbers that have a lowest common multiple of 40.

Key points

- Square numbers make a square pattern of dots.
  To find the square of a number, you multiply it by itself.
- A square root is a number that is multiplied by itself to
  produce a given number.
  Finding the square root is the inverse of squaring.
- Square numbers and roots are types of indices (powers) and you must use the
  priority of operations to do calculations. Use **BIDMAS**:
  Brackets → **I**ndices (powers) → **D**ivision and **M**ultiplication → **A**ddition and **S**ubtraction

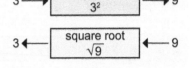

Purposeful practice 1

1 Work out each square number.

   a 1^2 **b** 2^2 **c** 3^2 **d** 4^2 **e** 5^2 **f** 6^2

   g 7^2 **h** 8^2 **i** 9^2 **j** 10^2 **k** 11^2 **l** 12^2

2 Each of these sequences of square numbers is missing a value. Write each missing value.

   a 1, ☐, 9, 16, 25   **b** 9, 16, 25, ☐, 49

   c 49, ☐, 81, 100   **d** 81, 100, ☐, 144

Reflect and reason

Jean writes $15^2 = 30$.

What mistake has she made?

What is the answer to 15^2?

Purposeful practice 2

Work out

   1 $\sqrt{49}$ **2** $\sqrt{16}$ **3** $\sqrt{144}$ **4** $\sqrt{36}$ **5** $\sqrt{64}$

   6 $\sqrt{1}$ **7** $\sqrt{25}$ **8** $\sqrt{100}$ **9** $\sqrt{121}$ **10** $\sqrt{81}$

Reflect and reason

Write 'square' or 'square root' to complete these sentences.

9 is the _____ of 3.

3 is the _____ of 9.

81 is the _____ of 9.

Purposeful practice 3

Work out each calculation.

   1 a $5^2 + 3$ **b** $5^2 + 3^2$ **c** $(5 + 3)^2$

   　d $9^2 - 4$ **e** $9^2 - 4^2$ **f** $(9 - 4)^2$

   　g $9^2 \div 3$ **h** $9^2 \div 3^2$ **i** $(9 \div 3)^2$

2 **a** $4 \times 2^2 + 3$ **b** $4 \div 2^2 + 3$ **c** $2^2 + 3 \times 4$

     d $3^2 - 4 \div 2$ **e** $4 \times (2^2 + 3)$ **f** $(4 \div 2)^2 + 3$

     g $(2 + 3)^2 \times 4$ **h** $(4^2 - 3^2) \times 4$ **i** $(4 - 3)^2 \times 4$

Reflect and reason

Miguel says, '$6^2 - 5^2$ and $(6 - 5)^2$ give the same answer.' Explain why Miguel is wrong.

☒ Problem-solving practice

1 Copy and complete each calculation.

     a $\square^2 = 25$ **b** $\square^2 = 49$ **c** $\square^2 = 121$

     d $\sqrt{\square} = 2$ **e** $\sqrt{\square} = 8$ **f** $\sqrt{\square} = 9$

2 Here are some numbers.

     $\sqrt{81}$ 3 3^2 $\sqrt{49}$ 27   9

     Write down three values from the list that are equal.

3 Here are some numbers.

     1, 2, 4, 6, 9, 12, 16, 18, 20

     Choose two square numbers that total

     a 10   **b** 20

     Nick says, 'The answer to part **a** is 4 and 6.'

     c Explain why Nick is incorrect.

4 Can 55 dots make a square pattern with none left over? Explain your answer.

5 Mandip has 90 square tiles.

     a Mandip makes the biggest possible solid square she can make out of these tiles. How many tiles make up one side of this square?

     b How many tiles will Mandip have left over?

6 Copy and complete each calculation.

     a $\square^2 + 3^2 = 90$ **b** $\square^2 + \sqrt{9} = 84$ **c** $\square^2 + \sqrt{9} = 19$

     d $\sqrt{81} - \square^2 = 0$ **e** $\sqrt{81} \times \sqrt{\square} = 18$ **f** $10^2 \div \square^2 = 4$

7 Consecutive numbers are numbers that follow each other in order.

     Chloe thinks of two consecutive numbers.

     She squares both numbers.

     The total of these two square numbers is 25.

     What were Chloe's two numbers?

8 Dominic thinks of two consecutive numbers between 10 and 15.

     He squares both numbers.

     The difference between these two square numbers is 25.

     What were Dominic's two numbers?

9 Frederika thinks of two consecutive multiples of 2.

     She squares both numbers.

     The total of the two square numbers is 100.

     What were Frederika's two numbers?

3.1 Functions

Key point

- A function is a relationship between two sets of numbers. The numbers that go into a function machine are called the inputs. The numbers that come out are called the outputs.

△ Purposeful practice 1

1 Work out the output of each function machine.

a input 12 → (+4) → output ☐   **b** input 12 → (×4) → output ☐

c input 12 → (−4) → output ☐   **d** input 12 → (÷4) → output ☐

2 Write two possible functions for each function machine.

a input 20 → output 10   **b** input 10 → output 20   **c** input 30 → output 10

d input 10 → output 30   **e** input 30 → output 5   **f** input 5 → output 20

3 Write the function for each function machine.

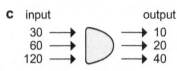

a
input	output
20	10
50	40
90	80

b
input	output
10	20
11	22
12	24

c
input	output
30	10
60	20
120	40

d
input	output
5	20
8	23
11	26

Reflect and reason

Dan says, 'The function for this function machine is × 4.'
Explain why Dan is wrong.

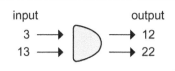

input	output
3	12
13	22

△ Purposeful practice 2

Work out the outputs of each two-step function machine.

1 input 1, 3, 6 → (×2) → (+4) → output ☐

2 input 1, 3, 6 → (+4) → (×2) → output ☐

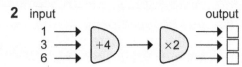

3

input → ×4 → +2 → output
1, 3, 6

4

input → +2 → ×4 → output
1, 3, 6

5

input → ÷2 → +4 → output
8, 10, 12

6

input → +4 → ÷2 → output
8, 10, 12

7

input → ÷2 → −4 → output
8, 10, 12

8

input → −4 → ÷2 → output
8, 10, 12

Reflect and reason

For any input number, do these function machines both give the same output number?
Choose three input numbers to show your working.

input → +2 → ×2 → output   and   input → ×2 → +2 → output

⊠ Problem-solving practice

1 Jill is asked to write the function for this function machine.
Jill writes +10
  a Explain why Jill is wrong.
  b Write the correct function.

input   output
5 → → 15
7 → → 21

2 For each pair of function machines, can you find an input number that gives the same output in both machines?
If you can, write the input and output.

  a input → ×4 → output   and   input → +6 → output

  b input → −4 → output   and   input → ÷2 → output

3 Abi, James and Sanjeev are all asked what the function is for this function machine.
Abi says, 'The function is divide by 4.'
James says, 'The function is subtract 6.'
Sanjeev says, 'The function is one quarter.'
Who is correct and who is incorrect? Explain your answer.

input   output
8 → → 2
20 → → 5
60 → → 15

4 Kayleigh has smudged her work after completing a function machine.
Copy and complete the function machine by working out the smudged numbers.
If you cannot be sure about any numbers, suggest what they might be.

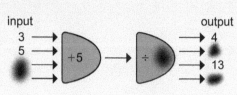

input → +5 → ÷ → output
3, 5   4, 13

Key points

- Like terms contain the same letter (or contain no letter). For example, $5x$ and $7x$ are like terms, but $4x$ and $3y$ are not like terms.
- You simplify an expression by collecting like terms.

△ Purposeful practice 1

1 Simplify

a $x + x$ **b** $x + x + x$ **c** $2x + x$ **d** $x + 2x$

e $x + 2x + x$ **f** $x + 3x$ **g** $3x + x$ **h** $3x + 2x$

i $3x + 2x + x$ **j** $4x + 2x$ **k** $4x + 2x + x$ **l** $2x + 5x$

2 Simplify

a $x - x$ **b** $2x - x$ **c** $3x - x$ **d** $3x - 2x$

e $3x - 3x$ **f** $4x - 3x$ **g** $4x - 2x$ **h** $4x - x$

3 Work out

a $1 - 2$ **b** $1 - 3$ **c** $1 - 4$ **d** $1 - 5$

e $2 - 5$ **f** $2 - 4$ **g** $2 - 3$ **h** $2 - 2$

4 Simplify

a $x - 2x$ **b** $x - 3x$ **c** $x - 4x$ **d** $x - 5x$

e $2x - 5x$ **f** $2x - 4x$ **g** $2x - 3x$ **h** $2x - 2x$

Reflect and reason

Is $2x + 5x$ the same as $5x + 2x$? Explain your answer.

Is $2x - 5x$ the same as $5x - 2x$? Explain your answer.

△ Purposeful practice 2

Simplify each expression by collecting like terms.

1 a $x + x + 3$ **b** $3 + x + x$ **c** $x + 3 + x$

d $2x + x + 3$ **e** $3 + 2x + x$ **f** $2x + 3 + x$

g $3x + 5 + 4$ **h** $4 + 3x + 5$ **i** $5 + 3x + 4$

2 a $3y - y + 1$ **b** $1 + 3y - y$ **c** $3y + 1 - y$

d $5y - 3y + 2$ **e** $2 + 5y - 3y$ **f** $5y + 2 - 3y$

g $5y - 3 + 2$ **h** $-3 + 5y + 2$ **i** $-3 + 2 + 5y$

3 a $2t + 5t + 3 + 1$ **b** $2t + 3 + 1 + 5t$ **c** $2t + 3 + 5t + 1$

d $2t + 5t + 3 - 1$ **e** $2t + 3 - 1 + 5t$ **f** $2t + 3 + 5t - 1$

4 a $2a + 5a + 3b + b$ **b** $2a + 3b + b + 5a$ **c** $2a + 3b + 5a + b$

d $2a + 5a + 3b - b$ **e** $2b + 3b - b + 5a$ **f** $2a + 3b + 5a - a$

5   **a** $3c - 5c + 2 + 4$ **b** $3c + 2 + 4 - 5c$ **c** $3c + 2 - 5c + 4$

       d $3c - 5c + 2d + 4d$ **e** $3c + 2d + 4d - 5c$ **f** $3c + 2d - 5c + 4d$

Reflect and reason

Jay writes

$5x - 3 + 2x = 5x - 2x + 3$

Who is correct? Explain why.

Lou writes

$5x - 3 + 2x = 5x + 2x - 3$

⊠ Problem-solving practice

1   Write three expressions that simplify to $12x$.

2   Copy and complete the magic square.
Every row, column and the two diagonals total $30n$.

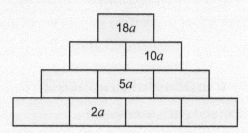

3   Which of these expressions simplify to $8x$? Write all that apply.

$6x + 2x$ $6x - 2x$ $2x + 4x + 2x + x$ $10x - 2x$ $2x - 10x$ $x + 8x$

4   Copy and complete this addition pyramid.
The term in any brick is the sum of the terms
in the two bricks directly below.

5   Sara and Alex are asked to simplify $8x + 6y - 5x + 2y$
Sara writes

$8x + 6y - 5x + 2y = 13x + 4y$

Sara says, 'I am right because there is a minus sign after $6y$, so take $2y$ from $6y$ and add the x's.'
Alex writes

$8x + 6y - 5x + 2y = 3x + 8y$

Alex says, 'I am right because there is a minus sign before $5x$, so take $5x$ from $8x$ and add the y's.'
Who is correct? Explain why.

6   Copy and complete this addition pyramid.
The expression in any brick is the sum of the
expressions in the two bricks directly below.

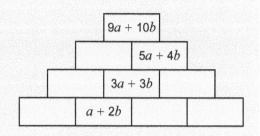

Key point

- To multiply out or expand expressions with brackets, multiply every number inside the brackets by the number outside the brackets.

△ Purposeful practice 1

Simplify each expression.

1 **a** $1 \times x$ **b** $2 \times x$ **c** $3 \times x$ **d** $x \times 5$
   e $x \times 4$ **f** $x \times 3$ **g** $n \times x$ **h** $x \times y$

2 **a** $1 \times 2y$ **b** $2 \times 2y$ **c** $3 \times 2y$ **d** $2y \times 5$
   e $2y \times 4$ **f** $2y \times 3$ **g** $2y \times 2$ **h** $2y \times 1$

3 **a** $a \times b$ **b** $b \times c$ **c** $c \times d$ **d** $d \times e$
   e $e \times d$ **f** $d \times c$ **g** $c \times b$ **h** $b \times a$

4 **a** $p \times p$ **b** $q \times q$ **c** $r \times r$ **d** $s \times s$

Reflect and reason

Explain what is wrong with these simplifications.

$t \times 7 = t7$ $t \times m = tm$ $n \times n = 2n$

△ Purposeful practice 2

Expand each expression.

1 **a** $2(x + 1)$ **b** $2(x + 2)$ **c** $2(x + 3)$ **d** $2(x + 4)$

2 **a** $3(x + 1)$ **b** $3(x + 2)$ **c** $3(x + 3)$ **d** $3(x + 4)$

3 **a** $4(y + 1)$ **b** $4(y + 2)$ **c** $4(y + 3)$ **d** $4(y + 4)$

4 **a** $2(x - 1)$ **b** $2(x - 2)$ **c** $2(x - 3)$ **d** $2(x - 4)$

5 **a** $3(x - 1)$ **b** $3(x - 2)$ **c** $3(x - 3)$ **d** $3(x - 4)$

6 **a** $4(y - 1)$ **b** $4(y - 2)$ **c** $4(y - 3)$ **d** $4(y - 4)$

7 **a** $3(2x + 1)$ **b** $3(2x + 2)$ **c** $3(2x + 5)$ **d** $3(2x + 10)$
   e $3(2x - 1)$ **f** $3(2x - 2)$ **g** $3(2x - 5)$ **h** $3(2x - 10)$

8 **a** $4(5y + 1)$ **b** $4(5y + 2)$ **c** $4(5y + 3)$ **d** $4(5y + 10)$
   e $4(5y - 1)$ **f** $4(5y - 2)$ **g** $4(5y - 3)$ **h** $4(5y - 10)$

Reflect and reason

When you expand $2(x + 5)$ and $2(x - 5)$, what is the same and what is different?

When you expand $3(y + 2)$ and $3(y + 4)$, what is the same and what is different?

⊠ Problem-solving practice

1 The term in each square comes from multiplying the terms in the two circles that are linked to the square. Copy and complete the diagram.

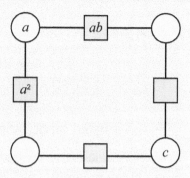

2 Write two multiplication calculations that give the answer $12n$.

3 Copy and complete the multiplication pyramid. Each brick is the product of the two bricks directly below.

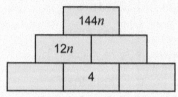

4 Amelia is asked to simplify $n \times n$.
Amelia writes
$$n \times n = nn$$
Amelia has not written her answer in the form normally used.
How should Amelia have written her answer?

5 Kevin and Jason are asked to expand $3(4y + 5)$.
Kevin writes
$$3(4y + 5) = 12y + 5$$

Jason writes
$$3(4y + 5) = 7y + 8$$

Both Kevin and Jason are incorrect.
a Explain what Kevin has done wrong.
b Explain Jason's mistake.
c Write the correct answer.

6 Match these expressions into equivalent pairs.

$3(4x - 3)$	$4(x - 3)$	$3(x - 4)$	$4(x + 3)$
$4(3x + 4)$	$3(4x + 3)$	$3(x + 4)$	$4(3x - 4)$
$4x - 12$	$12x - 9$	$12x - 16$	$3x - 12$
$4x + 12$	$12x + 9$	$3x + 12$	$12x + 16$

7 Copy and complete each calculation.
a $3(a + 7) = 3a + \square$ **b** $2(b + \square) = 2b + 6$ **c** $5(2b + \square) = \square + 20$

Key points

- You write an algebraic expression by using letters to stand for numbers.
- The letter is called a variable because its value can change or vary.

△ Purposeful practice 1

Write algebraic expressions for each description.

1 **a** 2 more than x **b** 2 less than x **c** 2 lots of x
    d twice x **e** double x **f** half of x

2 **a** 3 less than x **b** 3 lots of x **c** 3 more than x
    d one third of x **e** 3 subtract x **f** 3 add x

3 **a** 4 lots of x **b** 4 plus x more **c** 4 fewer than x
    d 4 times as much as x **e** one quarter of x **f** x multiplied by 4

4 **a** x with 5 added **b** 5 decreased by x **c** 5 less than x
    d 5 lots of x **e** x subtracted from 5 **f** x divided by 5

Reflect and reason

For 'twice x', Tim incorrectly writes the expression
$x + 2$.
Explain what Tim has done wrong.

△ Purposeful practice 2

1 Work out the sum of
    a 2 and 9 **b** 3 and 7 **c** 12 and 5 **d** 11 and 4

2 Work out the difference between
    a 2 and 9 **b** 3 and 7 **c** 12 and 5 **d** 11 and 4

3 Work out the product of
    a 2 and 9 **b** 3 and 7 **c** 12 and 5 **d** 11 and 4

4 Write an expression for the sum of
    a $2x$ and 9 **b** $3x$ and 7 **c** $12x$ and 5 **d** $11x$ and 4

5 Write an expression for the difference between
    a $2x$ and 9 **b** $3x$ and 7 **c** $12x$ and 5 **d** $11x$ and 4

6 Write and simplify an expression for the product of
    a $2x$ and 9 **b** $3x$ and 7 **c** $12x$ and 5 **d** $11x$ and 4

7 Write an expression for the sum of
    a $2x$ and $9x$ **b** $3x$ and $7x$ **c** $12x$ and $5x$ **d** $11x$ and $4x$

8 Write an expression for the difference between

   a $2x$ and $9x$ **b** $3x$ and $7x$ **c** $12x$ and $5x$ **d** $11x$ and $4x$

Reflect and reason

Liu writes $2x + 9 = 11x$

Explain the mistake Liu has made.

⊠ Problem-solving practice

1 Match each statement to its correct expression.

10 more than n		$10 - n$
10 less than n		$n - 10$
n subtracted from 10		$10n$
10 lots of n		$n + 10$

2 Sweets are sold in jars.
There are 80 sweets in a jar.
Akram buys one jar of sweets.
He takes s sweets out of the jar.
Write down an expression, in terms of s, for the number of sweets left in the jar.

3 Harry is half of George's age.
George is y years old.
Write an expression for Harry's age in terms of y.

4 Nadia is 3 years older than Alfie.
Cara is 5 years older than Nadia.
Alfie is y years old.
Which expression is Cara's age in terms of y?
  A $\ 8 - y$ B $\ y - 8$ C $\ y + 8$ D $\ y + 2$

5 Evie is twice as old as Duncan.
Finn is 3 years younger than Evie.
Duncan is y years old.
Finn says, 'I am $2y + 3$ years old.'
  a Explain what Finn has done wrong.
  b What is Finn's age in terms of y?

6 Katie has p pets.
Daniel has twice as many pets as Katie.
Ellie has 5 more pets than Katie.
  a Write an expression, in terms of p, for the number of pets that Katie, Daniel and Ellie each have.
  b Write an expression, in terms of p, for the total number of pets that Katie, Daniel and Ellie have.

7 Simon and Shona both think of a number.
Shona's number is n.
Simon's number is 12 more than Shona's number.
Write an expression for the total of Simon and Shona's number.

Key point

- You can use a formula to work out an unknown value by substituting the values that you do know into the formula.

⚠ Purposeful practice 1

1 The letters A to F are given by these formulae.

$A = x + 2$ $B = x - 1$ $C = 12 - x$

$D = 2x$ $E = 6x$ $F = \dfrac{x}{2}$

Find the value of each letter A to F by substituting

  a $x = 10$ **b** $x = 2$ **c** $x = 3$

2 The letters G to L are given by these formulae.

$G = x + y$ $H = y - x$ $I = 5y$

$J = xy$ $K = \dfrac{y}{3}$ $L = \dfrac{y}{x}$

Find the value of each letter G to L by substituting

  a $x = 1, y = 3$ **b** $x = 3, y = 6$

  c $x = 4, y = 12$ **d** $x = 2, y = 0$

Reflect and reason

Sam substitutes $a = 3$ and $b = 5$ into $x = ab$. Sam writes $x = 35$.
Explain what Sam has done wrong.

⚠ Purposeful practice 2

1 Substitute $n = 20$ into each formula to find the values of letters M to W.

$M = n + 100$ $P = n + 30$ $Q = n + 10$

$R = 2n + 10$ $S = 3n + 10$ $T = 3n + 20$

$U = 3n - 10$ $V = 5n - 10$ $W = 5n + 7$

2 Substitute $t = 6$ into each formula to find the values of letters a to h.

$a = 2t$ $b = 3t$ $c = 5t$ $d = 5t + 4$

$e = 5t + 10$ $f = 5t - 2$ $g = 4t - 2$ $h = 4t + 6$

3 Substitute $a = 4$ and $b = 0$ into each formula to find the values of letters i to n.

$i = 2a + b$ $j = 4a - b$ $k = a + 2b$

$l = 5a + 2b$ $m = 5a - 3b$ $n = 10a - 3b$

4 Substitute $a = 7$ and $b = 2$ into each formula to find the values of letters p to w.

$p = a + b$ $q = 2a + b$ $r = 3a - b$ $s = 3a + 2b$

$t = 3a - 2b$ $u = 5a + 3b$ $v = 5a - 3b$ $w = 3a - 5b$

Reflect and reason

$z = 2x + 3y$

Explain how you use the priority of operations to find the value of z if $x = 4$ and $y = 6$.

---

1   Malik is asked to substitute $a = 7$ and $b = 2$ into $x = 5a - 3b$
    Malik writes
    $x = 57 - 32 = 25$
    a Explain what Malik has done wrong.
    b Work out the correct answer.

2   Nick is asked to substitute $x = 4$ and $y = 3$ into $T = 10x + 7y$
    Nick writes
    $T = 10 \times 4 + 7 \times 3 = 40 + 7 \times 3 = 47 \times 3 = 141$
    a Explain what Nick has done wrong.
    b Work out the correct answer.

3   The equation of a straight line is $y = 4x + 3$
    Work out the value of y when $x = 5$

4   The formula to work out the average speed, s, is
    $$s = \frac{d}{t}$$
    where d is the distance travelled and t is the time taken.
    Work out the average speed for a journey that is 200 km and takes 4 hours.

5   The formula to work out the area, A, of a parallelogram is
    $A = bh$
    where b is the base and h is the height of the parallelogram.
    Work out the area of a parallelogram with a base 10 cm and height 8 cm.

6   For the formula $P = 3a - 2b$, decide whether each statement is true or false and
    explain your answer.
    a When $a = 6$ and $b = 5$, P is even.
    b When $a = 5$ and $b = 0$, P is negative.
    c When $a = 0$ and $b = 5$, P is negative.
    d There are no values for a and b that mean P will be odd.
    e P is always less than 50.

7   Using the values $p = 10$ and $q = 0$, which of these formulae
    a gives the greatest value for X
    b give the same value for X?

$X = pq$	$X = p + q$	$X = p - q$
$X = 5p - 20q$	$X = 100q$	$X = \dfrac{q}{p}$

8   Using the values $x = 7$ and $y = 5$, which formulae give an even value for A?

$A = x + y$	$A = xy$	$A = 8x - 3y$
$A = x - y$	$A = 3x$	$A = 4x + 6y$

Key point

- You can write a formula in words to work out an amount, then use letters to represent the variables.

△ Purposeful practice 1

1 **a** Work out the number of days, d, in

    i 1 week   **ii** 3 weeks

  b Write a formula for the number of days, d, in w weeks.

2 **a** Work out the number of weeks, w, in

    i 14 days   **ii** 56 days

  b Write a formula for the number of weeks, w, in d days.

3 **a** Work out the number of minutes, m, in

    i 5 hours   **ii** 10 hours

  b Write a formula for the number of minutes, m, in x hours.

4 **a** Work out the number of hours, h, in

    i 120 minutes   **ii** 240 minutes

  b Write a formula for the number of hours, h, in t minutes.

5 Write a formula for the number of legs for different numbers of

  a humans (2 legs each) (this has been started for you)

    Number of legs = number of humans × ☐

$$L = h \times \square$$
$$L = \square h$$

  b cats (4 legs each)   **c** ants (6 legs each)   **d** spiders (8 legs each)

Reflect and reason

For **Q5**, Dom wrote this formula for number of legs on c cats: $L = 4c$

Jane wrote this formula for number of legs on n cats: $L = 4n$

Do both formulae give the same value of L for 10 cats?

Does it matter which letter you use in a formula?

△ Purposeful practice 2

1 Write a formula for the number of legs L when there are

  a x humans and one cat   **b** x humans and y cats

  c x humans and z cats   **d** one ant and z cats

  e one ant and z spiders   **f** n ants and z spiders

  g z spiders and one human   **h** z spiders and f ants

  i z spiders and g ants   **j** k cats and g ants

2 In a café, £T is the price of tea and £C is the price of coffee.
Write a formula for the total price £P of

a 1 tea and 1 coffee   **b** 2 teas   **c** 3 coffees

d 2 teas and 1 coffee   **e** 2 teas and 3 coffees   **f** 4 teas and 1 coffee

g 3 teas and 1 coffee   **h** 2 teas and a £1 tip   **i** 2 teas and a £2 tip

j 3 coffees with £1 off   **k** 3 coffees with £2 off   **l** 2 teas with £1 discount

---

Reflect and reason

In a café, £T is the price of tea and £C is the price of coffee.

Which formula is correct for 4 teas, 1 coffee and a £2 tip? Explain your answer.

A $P = 4T + C - 2$ B $P = 4C + T + 2$

C $P = 4T + C + 2$ D $P = 4C + T - 2$

⊠ Problem-solving practice

1 Write a formula for the total length, L, in terms of x for the line below.

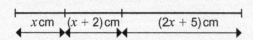

2 Mrs Koo asks her class to write a formula for the total cost, £P, of 3 cookies at £c each, 2 cups of tea at £t each, and a £1 tip.

Student A writes   Student B writes   Student C writes

$P = 3c + 2t + 1$ $P = 3t + 2c + 1$ $P = 3c + 2t - 1$

Which student has written the correct formula? Explain your answer.

3 Sweets cost s pence per packet and crisps cost c pence per bag.
Alan buys 4 packets of sweets, 3 bags of crisps and an 80p chocolate bar.
Write down a formula for how much Alan spends.

4 A company sell pencils in boxes and in packets.
There are b pencils in each box and p pencils in each packet.
A school buys 8 boxes of pencils and 3 packets of pencils.

a Write a formula for the total number of pencils the school buys.

The cost of a box of pencils is £X and the cost of a packet of pencils is £Y.

b Write a formula for the total cost of the pencils the school buys.

5 Minced beef is sold in small and large packs.
There are 400 g in a small pack.
There are 750 g in a large pack.
Chloe buys s small packs of minced beef and l large packs of minced beef.

a Write a formula for how much minced beef Chloe has.

Sabrina buys a small packs of minced beef and b large packs of minced beef.
She is given an extra 250 g for free.

b Write a formula for how much minced beef Sabrina has.

Mixed exercises A

1 Nisha and Zach go shopping.

   a Nisha buys the coat and the T-shirt.
     Work out the total cost.

   b Zach buys two items of clothing.
     He pays with £70 and gets £7 change.
     Which two items did Zach buy?

2 Marco writes these lists of numbers.

   Multiples of 3: 1, 3, 27, 33, 45
   Factors of 36: 3, 4, 15, 16, 18
   Square numbers: 2, 4, 8, 81, 121

   a Which numbers has Marco put in the wrong list?

   b Which of the numbers in part **a** belong in one of the other lists? Which list should
     they be in?

3 Alice earns £9 for each hour she works from Monday to Friday.
   She earns £12 for each hour she works on Saturday.
   One week, Alice worked for 5 hours on Saturday.

   a How much did Alice earn on Saturday?

   Altogether in that week she earned £303.

   b How much did Alice earn from Monday to Friday?

   c How many hours did Alice work that week, including Saturday?

4 a Copy and complete the table for this two-step function
     machine.

input	output
1	1
4	
7	
	33

input → ×4 → −3 → output

   b Here is a different two-step function machine.
     When the input is 42, the output is 10.

     Copy and complete the function machine.

input → ÷6 → ☐ → output

5 Match each question part to the correct expression (labelled A to D) **and** the correct statement (labelled P to S).

a $7x + 6y$ **b** $6x + 7y$ **c** $7x - 6y$ **d** $6x - 7y$

    A $10x + 6y - 4x + y$ P   7 lots of y subtracted from 6 lots of x
    B $7x + 2y - x - 9y$ Q   7 lots of x plus 6 lots of y
    C $4x + 2y + 3x + 4y$ R   7 lots of x minus 6 lots of y
    D $6x + 5y + x - 11y$ S   The total of 6 lots of x and 7 lots of y

6 Simon is putting pencils into packets.
He has 9000 pencils. He puts 12 pencils in each packet.
Simon puts the packets of pencils into boxes. He puts 25 packets into each box.
Work out the total number of boxes Simon needs.
You must show your working.

7 Copy and complete each set of whole numbers.
Explain the method you use to work out the possible missing numbers.
a For ☐, ☐, ☐ the mode is 5 and the range is 4.
b For 11, ☐, ☐, 14 the median is 13.5.
c For ☐, ☐, ☐, ☐, ☐ the mode is 5, the median is 8 and the mean is 10.
d For ☐, ☐, 5 the mean is 0.

8 The bar-line chart shows the number of messages Montana sent on each of five days last week.
The pictogram shows the number of messages Lexi sent on the same five days.

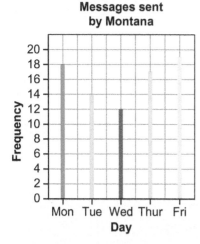

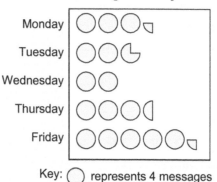

Key: ◯ represents 4 messages

a Who sent more messages during these five days?
Show your working to explain your answer.
b Draw a dual bar chart to show the number of messages Montana and Lexi sent.
c On which day did Lexi send more messages than Montana?

9 A shops sells crisps in small packets and large packets.
There are x small packets in a multipack and y large packets in a box.
A shop buys 12 multipacks and 5 boxes.
Zara is asked to write a formula for the total number of packets of crisps the shop buys.
Zara writes
$T = 17xy$
Is Zara correct? Explain your answer.

4 Decimals and measures

4.1 Decimals and rounding

Key points

- Digits after the decimal point represent fractions. You can see the value of each digit in a place value table.

H	T	U	·	$\frac{1}{10}$	$\frac{1}{100}$	$\frac{1}{1000}$
		0	·	1		
		0	·	0	1	
		0	·	0	0	1

$0.1 = \frac{1}{10}$ (one tenth)
$0.01 = \frac{1}{100}$ (one hundredth)
$0.001 = \frac{1}{1000}$ (one thousandth)

- For rounding to the nearest whole number, look at the tenths.
  0.5 and above round up.
  0.4 and below round down.

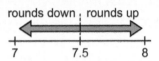

- A number written to 1 decimal place (1 d.p.) has only one digit after the decimal point.
- For rounding to 1 decimal place, look at the hundredths.
  0.05 and above round up.
  0.04 and below round down.

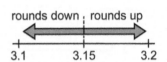

◬ Purposeful practice 1

1. What is the value of the digit 2 in each of these numbers?
   a 126.81   b 23.81   c 12.68   d 1.268
   e 1.026   f 1.206   g 0.120   h 0.102

Reflect and reason

Copy and complete ☐☐.☐☐☐ four times, using each of the digits 0, 1, 2, 3, 4 so that
a 2 has the greatest value
b 2 has the smallest value
c your number is greater than 43.201
d your number is equal to 43.12

◬ Purposeful practice 2

Round each number to
a the nearest whole number   b 1 decimal place

1 16.69   2 16.59   3 16.49   4 16.09   5 15.99
6 15.899   7 15.599   8 15.499   9 15.099   10 14.999

Reflect and reason

Which numbers give an answer of the same value when rounded to the nearest whole number as when rounded to 1 d.p.?

1 Estimate the answer to each of these calculations by rounding each number first.

   a 2.1×9.2 **b** 2.2×9.2 **c** 2.8×9.2

   d 2.9×9.2 **e** 2.9×9.8 **f** 2.9×9.86

   g 2.09×9.86 **h** 2.019×9.186 **i** 4.019×9.186

2 Estimate the answer to each of these calculations by rounding each number first.

   a $\sqrt{4.019} \times 9.186$ **b** $4.019 \times \sqrt{9.186}$ **c** $\sqrt{4.019} \times \sqrt{9.186}$

   d $4.019 \times \sqrt{99.186}$ **e** $99.186 \div 4.019$ **f** $99.186 \div \sqrt{4.019}$

   g $\sqrt{15.3} \times 3.15$ **h** $\sqrt{51.3} \times 1.35$ **i** $\sqrt{35.1} \times 5.31$

   j $14.3 \div 3.15$ **k** $51.3 \div 1.35$ **l** $34.1 \div 5.31$

Reflect and reason

How did you decide what to round the square rooted numbers to in **Q2** parts **g**, **h** and **i**?

How did you decide what to round the dividend (first number) to in **Q2** parts **j**, **k** and **l**?

⊠ **Problem-solving practice**

1 Alex is asked to round 7.99 to the nearest whole number.

Alex writes

$7.99 \approx 7.100$

Alex has written the answer incorrectly.

   a Explain Alex's mistake.

   b What is 7.9 rounded to the nearest whole number?

2 Fay says, 'The value of 7 in the number 45.678 is 7 hundreds.'

Is Fay correct? Explain why.

3 Which of these numbers give an answer of the same value when rounded to the nearest whole number as when rounded to 1 d.p.?

   23.92   23.96   24.03   24.07   24.23

4 Write a number that rounds to the value of 10 when rounded to the nearest whole number **and** when rounded to the nearest 1 d.p.

5 Will and Zannah are asked to work out an estimate to 4.09×7.8

Will writes

$4.09 \times 7.8 \approx 5 \times 8 = 40$

Zannah uses a calculator and writes

$4.09 \times 7.8 = 31.902$

Neither Will nor Zannah are correct.

   a Explain what mistake Will has made.

   b Explain what mistake Zannah has made.

   c Write a correct estimate to 4.09×7.8

6 Maria and Mohamed are asked to work out an estimate to $36.5 \div 4.03$

Maria says, '36.5 rounds to 37 and 4.03 rounds to 4 so an estimate is $37 \div 4 = 9.25$.'

Mohamed says, '36.5 rounds to 36 as a multiple of 4 and 4.03 rounds to 4 so an estimate is $36 \div 4 = 9$.'

Maria and Mohamed are both correct but one answer is a better estimate than the other. Who gave a better estimate? Explain your answer.

Key points

- When multiplying by 10, 100 or 1000, the digits move to the left. When dividing by 10, 100 or 1000, the digits move to the right. Use a place value table to help you.
- Metric units of length include the millimetre (mm), centimetre (cm), metre (m) and kilometre (km).
  10 mm = 1 cm, 100 cm = 1 m, 1000 m = 1 km
- Metric units of mass include the gram (g) and kilogram (kg).
  1000 g = 1 kg
- Metric units of capacity include the millilitre (ml) and litre.
  1000 ml = 1 litre

1.5×100
$150 \div 10$

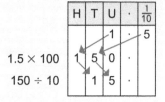

⚠ Purposeful practice 1

1 Work out

a 0.6×10	**b** 0.6×100	**c** 0.6×1000
d 0.06×10	**e** 0.06×100	**f** 0.06×1000
g 0.65×10	**h** 0.65×100	**i** 0.65×1000
j 0.605×10	**k** 0.065×10	**l** 6.005×100

2 Work out

a $7050 \div 10$	**b** $7050 \div 100$	**c** $7050 \div 1000$
d $961 \div 10$	**e** $961 \div 100$	**f** $961 \div 1000$
g $38 \div 10$	**h** $38 \div 100$	**i** $38 \div 1000$
j $1.7 \div 10$	**k** $1.7 \div 100$	**l** $0.17 \div 1000$

Reflect and reason

When multiplying a number by 10, 100 or 1000, is your answer smaller or larger than you started with?

When dividing a number by 10, 100 or 1000, is your answer smaller or larger than you started with?

⚠ Purposeful practice 2

1 Copy and complete these measurement conversions.
The first one has been done for you.

a 22 cm = 220 mm **b** 22 mm = ☐ cm

c 202 cm = ☐ mm **d** 202 mm = ☐ cm

e 202 cm = ☐ m **f** 202 m = ☐ cm

g 200 m = ☐ km **h** 200 km = ☐ m

i 2002 g = ☐ kg **j** 22 kg = ☐ g

k 20 ml = ☐ litres **l** 20 litres = ☐ ml

2 Write $<$ or $>$ between each pair of measures.

    a 44 cm ☐ 404 mm   **b** 404 m ☐ 4 km   **c** 909 m ☐ 0.9 km

    d 12.5 kg ☐ 1025 g   **e** 604 ml ☐ 0.64 litres

Reflect and reason

Coral says, 'When converting from a larger to a smaller unit of measure, you always divide, but when converting from a smaller to a larger unit of measure, you always multiply.'

Is Coral correct? Write two examples to support your answer.

⊠ Problem-solving practice

1 Li is asked to work out 4.7×10
Li writes $4.7 \times 10 = 0.47$

    a Explain the mistake Li has made.

    b What is 4.7×10?

2 Pete correctly measures the lengths of two lines A and B.
He writes
Line A = 63 mm
Line B = 6.5 cm
Pete says, 'Line A is longer because 63 is greater than 6.5.'
Pete is incorrect. Explain why.

3 A car boot is 1550 mm wide.
Will a post of length 160 cm fit across the boot? Give reasons for your answer.

4 Reema and Zara travel to the office for a meeting.
Reema travels 42 km to get there.
Zara travels 42 000 m to get there.
Zara says, 'I have travelled further as 42 000 is more than 42.'
Is Zara correct? Explain your answer.

5 A bucket has a capacity of 10 litres.
A jug has a capacity of 500 ml.
Sharon fills the jug with water and pours it into the bucket.
How many times must Sharon do this to fill the bucket?
You must show your working.

6 Clara has a 2 litre bottle of lemonade.
Clara is pouring the lemonade into glasses. Each glass holds 250 ml of lemonade.
How many glasses does Clara need to use all of the lemonade?
You must show your working.

7 The table shows the heights of some buildings.

Building	Height (metres)
Burj Khalifa	830
Shanghai Tower	632
Empire State Building	381
The Shard	310

Which of the buildings are more than half a kilometre high?

Key points

- When finding values on a scale, it can be helpful to find the halfway value first. When there is no halfway value, count the number of equal intervals between numbers that are marked. Use division to work out what value each interval represents.
- A decimal measure can be written using two units of measure.
  For example, 1.5 m = 1 m 50 cm

⚠ Purposeful practice 1

1 Write the number the arrow on each scale points to.

a
```
0                    ↑              60
```

b
```
0          ↑                       60
```

c
```
0              ↑                   60
```

d
```
0          ↑                       60
```

e
```
0    ↑                             60
```

f
```
0                ↑                 60
```

2 Write the measure the arrow on each scale points to.

a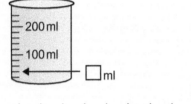

b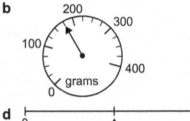

c

d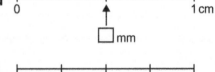

e

f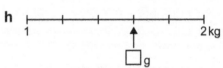

g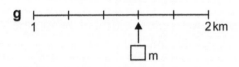

h
```
1                ↑                 2 kg
```
☐ g

i
```
1                    ↑             2 litres
```
☐ ml

Reflect and reason

Write instructions for a friend to help them find the value the arrow is pointing to on this scale.

Copy and complete

1 4.2 cm = ☐ cm ☐ mm   **2** 4.3 cm = ☐ cm ☐ mm   **3** 4.2 m = ☐ m ☐ cm

4 4.3 m = ☐ m ☐ cm   **5** 4.31 m = ☐ m ☐ cm   **6** 4.32 m = ☐ m ☐ cm

7 4.3 km = ☐ km ☐ m   **8** 4.35 km = ☐ km ☐ m   **9** 4.358 km = ☐ km ☐ m

Reflect and reason

Look at your answers to **Q2**, **Q4** and **Q7**. Explain why your answers are different each time.

⊠ **Problem-solving practice**

1 Jo is asked for the number the arrow is pointing to.
Jo says, 'The arrow is pointing at the number 2
because it is 2 divisions on from 0.'

   a Explain why Jo is incorrect.

   b What number is the arrow pointing to?

2 Which of these diagrams shows the arrow pointing to the smallest value?
Explain how you decided.

A
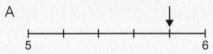

B

C
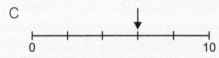

D
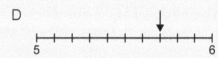

3 Which of these diagrams shows the arrow pointing to the longest length?
Explain how you decided.

A
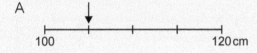

B

C
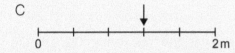

D
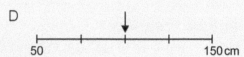

4 Almira works out 1.4 metres × 3 using her calculator.
The calculator shows the correct answer of 4.2
She is asked to write the answer in metres and centimetres.
Almira writes

1.4 m × 3 = 4.2 m = 4 m and 2 cm

   a Explain why Almira's answer is incorrect.

   b What answer should Almira have written?

5 Rob cycles 1.25 km to his friend Neil's house.
Rob says, 'I have cycled 1 kilometre and 25 metres to get here.'
Neil says, 'You have cycled 1 kilometre and 250 metres to get here.'
Who is correct? Explain your answer.

6 A cupboard is 1.2 m wide.
Will a stick 1 m 5 cm long fit across the cupboard?
Give reasons for your answer.

Key points

- You can use multiplication facts to work out decimal multiplications.
- You can use partitioning to work out decimal multiplications.
- You can use an answer to a decimal multiplication to work out the answer to related decimal multiplications.

△ Purposeful practice 1

Work out each calculation.

1 **a** 4×0.2 **b** 0.4×0.2 **c** 0.04×2
    d 2×0.4 **e** 0.2×0.4 **f** 0.02×4
    g 8×0.3 **h** 0.8×0.3 **i** 0.08×3
    j 3×0.8 **k** 0.3×0.8 **l** 0.03×8

2 **a** 12×0.5 **b** 0.12×0.5 **c** 0.012×5
    d 5×0.12 **e** 0.5×0.12 **f** 0.05×12

Reflect and reason

Why do **Q1** parts **b** and **e** give the same answer?

Why do **Q1** parts **i** and **l** give the same answer?

Dan says, 'The answer to **Q2e** is 0.6.' What do you think he has done wrong?

△ Purposeful practice 2

Work out

1 30×1.3 **2** 32×1.3 **3** 70×1.1 **4** 78×1.1
5 20×5.1 **6** 26×5.1 **7** 40×6.2 **8** 42×6.2

Reflect and reason

How did your answers to **Q1**, **Q3**, **Q5** and **Q7** help you find the answers to **Q2**, **Q4**, **Q6** and **Q8** respectively?

△ Purposeful practice 3

1 $0.71 \times 24 = 17.04$
    Use this fact to work out
    a 0.71×240 **b** 0.71×2.4 **c** 7.1×24
    d 7.1×2.4 **e** 7.1×240 **f** 71×240

2 $3.6 \times 0.8 = 2.88$
    Use this fact to work out
    a 3.6×8 **b** 3.6×0.08 **c** 0.36×0.8
    d 36×0.8 **e** 36×0.08 **f** 360×0.08

Reflect and reason

Why do **Q2** parts **d** and **f** give the same answer as **Q2a**?

1 Luca is asked to work out 0.3×0.1
Luca writes
$0.3 \times 0.1 = 0.3$
Luca's answer is incorrect.
  a Explain Luca's mistake.
  b What is 0.3×0.1?

2 Hannah is asked to work out 0.5×0.6
Hannah writes
$0.5 \times 0.6 = 0.3$
Is Hannah correct? Give a reason for your answer.

3 Decide whether each of these calculations has been worked out correctly.
Give reasons for your answer and if it's wrong, work out the correct answer.
  a $43 \times 1.1 = 40 \times 1.1 + 1.1$
  $\qquad\qquad = 44 + 1.1$
  $\qquad\qquad = 45.1$

  b $32 \times 1.4 = 30 \times 1.4 + 2 \times 1.4$
  $\qquad\qquad = 3 \times 10 \times 1.4 + 2.8$
  $\qquad\qquad = 42 + 2.8$
  $\qquad\qquad = 44.8$

4 Does 6.7×4.8 give the same answer as 670×0.48?
Give a reason for your answer.

5 $7 \times 0.26 = 1.82$
Use this fact to decide if these calculations are correct.
  a $7 \times 2.6 = 18.2$ **b** $0.7 \times 26 = 1.82$ **c** $0.7 \times 0.26 = 0.182$
  d $70 \times 2.6 = 182$ **e** $7 \times 26 = 182$ **f** $0.7 \times 0.026 = 0.182$

6 Copy and complete these calculations.
Use the fact $5.8 \times 0.6 = 3.48$
  a $58 \times \square = 3.48$ **b** $\square \times 6 = 3.48$ **c** $5.8 \times 0.06 = \square$
  d $0.58 \times \square = 3.48$ **e** $\square \times 6 = 348$ **f** $\square \times 0.6 = 0.348$

7 $4.2 \times 0.7 = 2.94$
Use this fact to write five other calculations and their answers.

8 Look at the calculations on the cards.
Which calculations give the same answer as 1.9×7.3?

| 19×7.3 | 0.19×73 | 19×0.73 | 0.019×730 |

| 0.19×7.3 | 1.9×73 | 190×0.73 | 1.9×0.73 |

9 Write four other calculations that give the same answer as 3.8×2.4

Key points

- You can use a zero place holder when adding or subtracting decimals with different numbers of decimal places. For example, you can write 45.9 − 23.45 as shown.

$$\begin{array}{r} 4\ 5\ .\ 9\ 0 \\ -\ 2\ 3\ .\ 4\ 5 \\ \hline \end{array}$$

- You can use the column method to multiply a decimal by a whole number, or vice versa.
- You can use short division to divide a decimal by a whole number.

△ Purposeful practice 1

1 Use a number line to work out

   a 3.4 + 2.5   **b** 3.4 + 2.6   **c** 3.4 + 2.7

   d 7.6 − 2.5   **e** 7.6 − 2.6   **f** 7.6 − 2.7

2 Work out

   a 4.4 + 2.5   **b** 4.4 + 2.6   **c** 4.4 + 2.7   **d** 5.4 + 2.7

   e 6.4 + 3.7   **f** 7.4 + 3.8   **g** 8.6 − 2.5   **h** 8.6 − 2.6

   i 8.6 − 2.7   **j** 8.6 − 3.7   **k** 8.7 − 3.7   **l** 8.7 − 3.8

3 Work out

   a 1.2 + 3.8   **b** 4.3 + 3.7   **c** 6.4 + 2.6   **d** 1.5 + 2.5

   e 1.6 + 4.4   **f** 1.7 + 1.3   **g** 7.8 + 2.2   **h** 5.9 + 3.1

4 Work out the missing numbers in these calculations.

   a 5 − 1.2 = ☐   **b** 8 − 3.7 = ☐   **c** 9 − 6.4 = ☐   **d** 4 − 2.5 = ☐

   e 6 − 1.6 = ☐   **f** 3 − 1.7 = ☐   **g** 10 − 3.8 = ☐   **h** 9 − 4.9 = ☐

Reflect and reason

How could you use your answer to **Q1a** to help you answer **Q1b**?

How could you use your answer to **Q1e** to help you answer **Q1f**?

Why are all the answers to **Q3** integers (whole numbers)?

△ Purposeful practice 2

1 Use the column method to work out

   a 24.27 + 31.52   **b** 24.27 + 1.63   **c** 24.27 + 9.6

   d 24.2 + 9.68   **e** 24.2 + 9.681   **f** 24.276 + 9.3

2 Use the column method to work out

   a 52.47 − 21.45   **b** 52.47 − 3.45   **c** 52.47 − 4.6

   d 52.4 − 4.58   **e** 52.47 − 4.581   **f** 52.4 − 4.581

Reflect and reason

Jon works out 92.7 − 3.68

What mistake has he made?

What is the correct answer?

$$\begin{array}{r} {}^{8}{}^{1}1 \\ \cancel{9}\ \cancel{2}.\overset{1}{7} \\ -\ 3\ .6\ 8 \\ \hline 5\ 5.9 \end{array}$$

1 Work out
   a 7.2×3 **b** 2.7×3 **c** 3.2×7 **d** 1.23×7 **e** 3×72.13

2 Work out
   a $80.4 \div 6$ **b** $46.4 \div 8$ **c** $184.8 \div 4$ **d** $148.02 \div 6$

Reflect and reason

Jenny works out 37.31×6
What two mistakes has she made?
What is the correct answer?

```
    3 7 3 1
  ×         6
    2 2 2 8 6
        4
```
$37.31 \times 6 = 2228.6$

⊠ **Problem-solving practice**

1 What is the total length of a car measuring 4.3 m and a trailer measuring 1.8 m?

2 Gemma and Sarah are meeting at the cinema.
   Gemma lives 2.6 km from the cinema.
   Sarah lives 4.5 km from the cinema.
   How much further than Gemma does Sarah have to travel to get to the cinema?

3 A car has a tank containing 45 litres of petrol.
   A journey uses 9.4 litres of the petrol.
   How much petrol is left in the tank?

4 Wendy is asked to work out $36.18 + 5.4$ using the column method.
   Wendy writes
```
    3 6.1 8
  + 5.4 0 0
    9 0.1 8
      1
```
   a Wendy is incorrect. What mistake has Wendy made?
   b What is the correct answer?

5 Lynne needs to post four parcels, each weighing 1.7 kg.
   Work out the total weight of the parcels.

6 Neveah has 3 lengths of ribbon.
   Each length is 1.8 m long.
   What length of ribbon does Neveah have in total?

7 A group of five friends go out for a meal.
   The bill comes to £72.80
   The bill is shared equally between the group.
   How much does each person pay?

8 Grace is asked to divide 64.2 by 6 using short division.
   Grace writes
```
      10.0
   6)64.2
```
   So $64.2 \div 6 = 10.0$
   a Grace is incorrect. What mistake has she made?
   b Work out the correct answer.

Key points

- The perimeter is the total distance around the edge of a shape. To work out the perimeter of any shape, add up the lengths of all the sides.
- A regular polygon is a straight-sided closed shape with all sides and all angles equal.

△ Purposeful practice 1

Work out the perimeters of these shapes.

1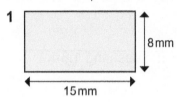

2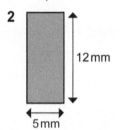

3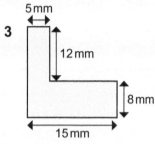

4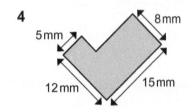

5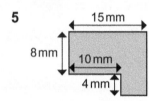

6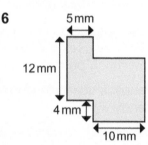

Reflect and reason

The shapes in **Q3** and **Q4** are both made up of the shapes in **Q1** and **Q2**. Why don't the shapes in **Q3** and **Q4** have the same perimeter?

△ Purposeful practice 2

Work out the perimeters of these regular polygons.

1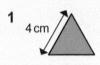

2

3

4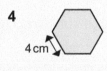

5

6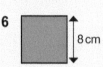

7

8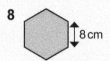

Reflect and reason

What do you notice about the perimeters of the polygons in **Q1** and **Q5**; **Q2** and **Q6**; **Q3** and **Q7**; **Q4** and **Q8**?

Predict the perimeter of a pentagon with side length 16 cm.

◭ Purposeful practice 3

Sara calls one side of this rectangle a cm.
Work out the perimeter when the other side length is

1 a cm

2 1 cm more than a

3 2 cm more than a

4 3 cm more than a

5 4 cm more than a

6 5 cm more than a

Reflect and reason

Copy and complete this sentence for the rectangle in Purposeful practice 3.

If one side length of a rectangle stays the same, and the other increases by 1 cm, then its perimeter increases by ___ cm.

⊠ Problem-solving practice

1 A square has perimeter 20 cm.
What is the length of the square?

2 This rectangle has perimeter 30 cm.
Work out the width of the rectangle.

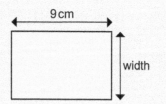

3 Tiff has a rectangle that measures 10 cm by 8 cm.
a Work out the perimeter of the rectangle.

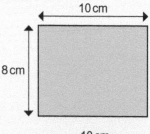

Tiff cuts a 3 cm square off the corner of the rectangle.
b Show that this shape has the same perimeter as the rectangle that Tiff started with. Explain why this happens.

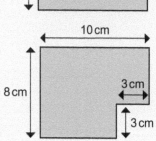

4 Tom is asked to work out the perimeter of this shape.
Tom writes

Perimeter = 6 + 12 + 9 + 5 = 32 cm

a Explain what Tom has done wrong.
b What is the correct perimeter of the shape?

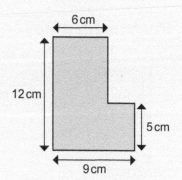

5 A regular hexagon has a perimeter of 72 cm.
Work out the length of each side of the hexagon.

Key points

- The area is the total space covered by a shape. You can find the area of a shape drawn on squared paper by counting the squares inside it.
  The units used for area are square units, such as mm^2, cm^2, m^2 and km^2.

  1 cm ▢ 1 cm has area $1\,cm^2$ 1 cm ◺ 1 cm is half a square, and it has an area of $0.5\,cm^2$

- To work out the area of a rectangle or square, use
    area = length × width
- To work out the area of a shape made of rectangles, it helps to split the shape into smaller rectangles.

△ Purposeful practice 1

Work out the area of each shape drawn on centimetre squared paper.

1
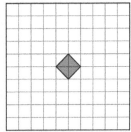

2
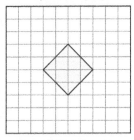

3
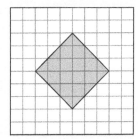

4
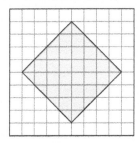

Reflect and reason

Write down the first four square numbers. How do the areas of these shapes relate to the square numbers? Explain why.

△ Purposeful practice 2

Work out the area of these shapes.

1
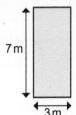

2
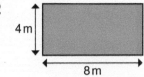

3
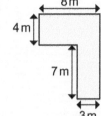

4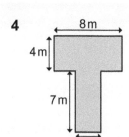

5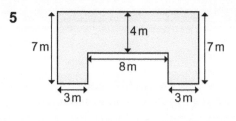

6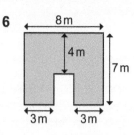

Reflect and reason

How can your answers to **Q1** and **Q2** help you find the answers to **Q3**, **Q4** and **Q5**?
Why can't your answers to **Q1** and **Q2** help you find the answer to **Q6**?

▲ Purposeful practice 3

Sara calls one side of this rectangle b.
Work out the area when the other side is

1 1 cm   **2** 2 cm

3 3 cm   **4** 4 cm   **5** 5 cm

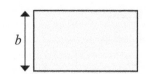

Reflect and reason

Copy and complete this sentence for the rectangle in Purposeful practice 3.

If one side of a rectangle stays the same length, b, and the other side increases by 1 cm
each time, then the area increases by _____ cm² each time.

⊠ Problem-solving practice

1 A square has an area of 49 cm². What is the length of the side of the square?

2 This rectangle has an area of 45 cm².
Work out the width of the rectangle.

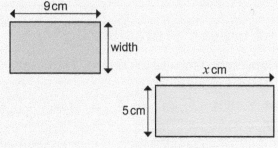

3 This rectangle has an area of 60 cm².
Work out the value of x.

4 Draw three different rectangles each with area 24 cm².

5 Freya is asked to work out the area of this shape.
Freya writes

Area = 6 × 12 + 9 × 5
     = 72 + 45
     = 117 cm²

a Explain what Freya has done wrong.
b What is the correct area of the shape?

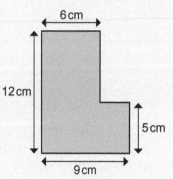

6 A rectangle has a width of 9 cm and an area of 108 cm².
Work out the length of the rectangle.

Key points

- It is important to be able to choose the most suitable units for measuring length, mass, capacity and area. The metric units you already know are
  Length: mm, cm, m, km   Mass: g, kg
  Capacity: ml, litre   Area: mm², cm², m², km²
- Some more metric units that you need to know are
  Mass: 1 tonne (t) = 1000 kg   Area: 1 hectare (ha) = 10 000 m²
  Capacity: 1 millilitre (ml) = 1 cm³
- You need to know these conversions between metric and imperial units.
  1 foot (ft) ≈ 30 cm   1 mile ≈ 1.6 km

△ Purposeful practice 1

Here are some units of measure.

km   tonnes   feet   hectares   cm³

Write the units you would you use to measure

1 the amount of water in a pond

2 the distance covered by a footpath

3 the length of a tree's branch

4 the amount of land covered by a forest

5 the mass of a fallen tree

Reflect and reason

How did you decide which unit of measure was suitable?

△ Purposeful practice 2

Copy and complete to convert these measures.

1 7t = ☐kg   **2** 7.1t = ☐kg   **3** 7.18t = ☐kg
4 7.189t = ☐kg   **5** 71.89t = ☐kg   **6** 4 litres = ☐cm³
7 4.2 litres = ☐cm³   **8** 4.26 litres = ☐cm³   **9** 4.263 litres = ☐cm³
10 42.63 litres = ☐cm³   **11** 9.3 hectares = ☐m²   **12** 9.35 hectares = ☐m²

Reflect and reason

Why do you need 0 in your answers to **Q1**, **Q2** and **Q3** but not **Q4**?

△ Purposeful practice 3

1 Copy and complete these measurement conversions.
    The first one has been done for you.

  a 70t = 70 000 kg   **b** 7000 kg = ☐t   **c** 0.3 ha = ☐m³
  d 300 m² = ☐ha   **e** 82 ml = ☐cm³   **f** 82 litres = ☐cm³

2 Copy and complete to convert these measures.

a 60 ft = ☐ cm   **b** 60 ft = ☐ m   **c** 60 cm = ☐ ft

d 60 mm = ☐ ft   **e** 10 miles = ☐ km   **f** 32 km = ☐ miles

---

Reflect and reason

How did you use your answer to **Q2a** to answer **Q2b**?

How did you use your answer to **Q2c** to answer **Q2d**?

⊠ Problem-solving practice

1 Tia has a box with a volume of 300 cm³.
Tia says, 'If I fill the box with water it will hold 0.3 litres of water.'
Is Tia correct? Explain your answer.

2 An elephant weighs 4.2 tonnes.
During a pregnancy the elephant gains 300 kg in weight.
What is the most the elephant weighs during pregnancy?
Give your answer in tonnes. You must show your working.

3 A farm covers an area of 32.5 hectares.
The farmer sells a field with an area of 8000 m².
What is the area of the farm now?
Give your answer in hectares.
You must show your working.

4 Sean measures the lengths of two lines.
He writes
Line A = 3 feet
Line B = 85 cm
Sean says, 'Line B is longer because 85 is greater than 3.'
Sean is incorrect. Explain why.

5 A shelf is 2 feet wide.
How many books, each 2 cm wide, will fit on the shelf?
You must show your working.

6 Emma and Yasmina compare the distances they travel to get to school.
Emma travels 3 km to get there.
Yasmina travels 2 miles to get there.
Yasmina says, 'I have travelled the least as 2 is less than 3.'
Is Yasmina correct? Explain your answer.

7 The table shows the heights of some buildings in the USA.
Write the buildings in height order, starting with the tallest.
You must show your working.

Building	Height
Bank of America Tower	1200 feet
Chrysler Building	318.9 metres
Empire State Building	381 metres
Willis Tower	1729 feet

8 A garage door is 10 feet wide.
Will a truck with a width 2.1 m fit through the garage door?
Explain your answer.

5 Fractions and percentages

5.1 Comparing fractions

Key points

- A fraction is part of a whole.
- The number above the line in a fraction is the numerator.
  The number below the line is the denominator.

  $\dfrac{1}{2}$ ← numerator
       ← denominator

- A unit fraction has numerator 1.

⚠ Purposeful practice 1

Copy the pairs of fractions and write the correct sign, < or >, between each pair.
You may use the fraction wall to help you.

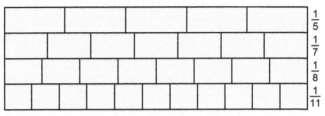

1 a $\frac{3}{5} \square \frac{2}{5}$ b $\frac{1}{5} \square \frac{3}{5}$ c $\frac{4}{5} \square \frac{3}{5}$

2 a $\frac{2}{7} \square \frac{3}{7}$ b $\frac{2}{7} \square \frac{1}{7}$ c $\frac{2}{7} \square \frac{6}{7}$ d $\frac{5}{7} \square \frac{6}{7}$

3 a $\frac{7}{8} \square \frac{3}{8}$ b $\frac{3}{8} \square \frac{5}{8}$ c $\frac{5}{8} \square \frac{1}{8}$ d $\frac{1}{8} \square \frac{6}{8}$

4 a $\frac{5}{11} \square \frac{8}{11}$ b $\frac{8}{11} \square \frac{10}{11}$ c $\frac{10}{11} \square \frac{4}{11}$ d $\frac{4}{11} \square \frac{7}{11}$

Reflect and reason

When the denominators are the same, how can you decide which fraction is larger?

⚠ Purposeful practice 2

1 Copy the pairs of fractions and write the correct sign, < or >, between each pair.
You may use the fraction wall to help you.

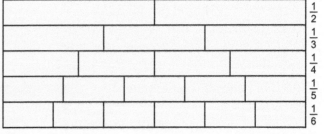

a $\frac{1}{2} \square \frac{1}{6}$ b $\frac{1}{4} \square \frac{1}{6}$ c $\frac{1}{4} \square \frac{1}{3}$ d $\frac{1}{5} \square \frac{1}{3}$ e $\frac{1}{5} \square \frac{1}{2}$ f $\frac{1}{4} \square \frac{1}{2}$

g $\frac{1}{4} \square \frac{1}{7}$ h $\frac{1}{9} \square \frac{1}{7}$ i $\frac{1}{9} \square \frac{1}{12}$ j $\frac{1}{13} \square \frac{1}{12}$ k $\frac{1}{13} \square \frac{1}{15}$ l $\frac{1}{5} \square \frac{1}{15}$

Reflect and reason

For unit fractions, how can you decide which fraction is larger?

1 Copy the pairs of fractions and write the correct sign, < or >, between each pair. You may use the fraction wall from Purposeful practice 2 to help you.

a $\frac{1}{2} \square \frac{2}{3}$ b $\frac{5}{6} \square \frac{2}{3}$ c $\frac{3}{4} \square \frac{2}{3}$ d $\frac{1}{3} \square \frac{1}{2}$ e $\frac{1}{3} \square \frac{2}{5}$ f $\frac{1}{3} \square \frac{2}{7}$

g $\frac{3}{5} \square \frac{3}{4}$ h $\frac{3}{5} \square \frac{3}{6}$ i $\frac{3}{5} \square \frac{3}{7}$ j $\frac{4}{7} \square \frac{4}{5}$ k $\frac{2}{3} \square \frac{2}{5}$ l $\frac{2}{7} \square \frac{2}{8}$

m $\frac{3}{4} \square \frac{4}{5}$ n $\frac{3}{4} \square \frac{5}{6}$ o $\frac{3}{4} \square \frac{4}{6}$

Reflect and reason

Look at your answers to parts **b**, **c** and **o**. Does the larger fraction always have a larger numerator?

Look at your answers to parts **f** and **o**. Does the smaller fraction always have a smaller numerator?

Problem-solving practice

1 During a game, Dan and Mark each spin a spinner the same number of times. The winner is the person whose spinner lands on A more times.

$\frac{1}{5}$ of Dan's spins land on A.

$\frac{1}{6}$ of Mark's spins land on A.

Mark says, 'I won because 6 is greater than 5.'
Is Mark correct? Explain your answer.

2 A bag is full of counters.

$\frac{3}{7}$ of the counters are red.

$\frac{3}{8}$ of the counters are blue.

Are there more red or blue counters? Explain your answer.

3 State whether each statement is true or false. Explain your answers.

a $\frac{3}{8} > \frac{5}{8}$ b $\frac{3}{8} > \frac{3}{10}$ c $\frac{3}{8} > \frac{2}{5}$

4 Use the bar to decide which is larger, $\frac{1}{3}$ or $\frac{5}{12}$

5 Ali says, '$\frac{3}{4}$ is less than $\frac{5}{8}$ because 5 and 8 are greater than 3 and 4.'

Is Ali correct? Explain your answer.

6 Kelly and Becky each have a box with the same total number of chocolates.

$\frac{3}{10}$ of Kelly's chocolates are white chocolates.

$\frac{2}{5}$ of Becky's chocolates are white chocolates.

Who has the most white chocolates?

7 Colin is asked to circle the lowest fraction in the box.

$\frac{3}{5}$ $\frac{5}{8}$ $\frac{1}{2}$

Colin circles $\frac{3}{5}$
Is Colin correct? Explain your answer.

Key points

- An improper fraction has a numerator bigger than its denominator, for example $\frac{3}{2}$
- A mixed number has a whole number part and a fraction part, for example $1\frac{1}{2}$
- Equivalent fractions have the same value. You can find equivalent fractions by multiplying or dividing the numerator and denominator by the same number.

△ Purposeful practice 1

1 Simplify

   a $\frac{2}{2}$ **b** $\frac{3}{3}$ **c** $\frac{6}{6}$ **d** $\frac{10}{10}$ **e** $\frac{56}{56}$ **f** $\frac{92}{92}$

2 Convert each improper fraction to a mixed number.

   a $\frac{3}{2}$ **b** $\frac{4}{3}$ **c** $\frac{7}{6}$ **d** $\frac{11}{10}$ **e** $\frac{57}{56}$ **f** $\frac{93}{92}$

   g $\frac{5}{2}$ **h** $\frac{7}{2}$ **i** $\frac{9}{2}$ **j** $\frac{5}{3}$ **k** $\frac{7}{3}$ **l** $\frac{8}{3}$

   m $\frac{8}{5}$ **n** $\frac{9}{5}$ **o** $\frac{11}{5}$ **p** $\frac{12}{5}$ **q** $\frac{13}{10}$ **r** $\frac{23}{10}$

Reflect and reason

Three students convert $\frac{10}{3}$ to a mixed number.

Sam writes   Liz writes   Jeff writes

$\frac{10}{3} = 1\frac{7}{3}$ $\frac{10}{3} = 2\frac{4}{3}$ $\frac{10}{3} = 3\frac{1}{3}$

Explain why their mixed numbers are all equivalent.

Whose answer is best? Why?

△ Purposeful practice 2

Find equivalent fractions using the multiplications given.

1 a 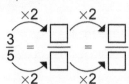   **b**

2 a 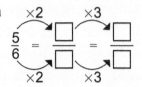   **b**

3 a 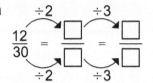   **b** 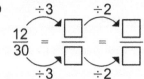   **c**

4 a 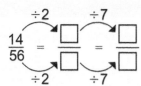 **b** 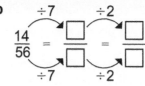 **c**

Reflect and reason

Matt says, 'To simplify a fraction, it doesn't matter which factor you divide by first.'
Use your answers from Purposeful practice 2 to show that Matt is correct.

What single multiplication is equivalent to ×2 then ×3?
Which two divisions are equivalent to ÷15?

⊠ Problem-solving practice

1 Seb is asked to convert $\frac{11}{4}$ to a mixed number. Seb writes

$\frac{11}{4} = 2\frac{3}{11}$

Explain the mistake Seb has made.

2 Kyle, Liz and Mel are asked to simplify $\frac{8}{20}$

Kyle writes   Liz writes   Mel writes

Who is correct? Explain your answer.

3 Ned is asked to simplify $\frac{12}{18}$. Ned writes

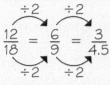

a Explain what Ned has done wrong.

b What is the correct answer?

4 Natalie is asked to write five equivalent fractions to $\frac{1}{2}$, using the smallest possible digits she can. Natalie writes

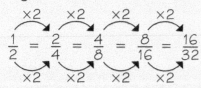

Natalie says, 'Using my workings, $\frac{1}{2}$, $\frac{2}{4}$, $\frac{4}{8}$, $\frac{8}{16}$ and $\frac{16}{32}$ are the five equivalent fractions to $\frac{1}{2}$ with the smallest possible digits.'

Natalie is incorrect. Explain why.

5 Sort these fractions into groups of equivalent fractions.

$\boxed{\frac{10}{25}}$ $\boxed{\frac{24}{32}}$ $\boxed{\frac{5}{15}}$ $\boxed{\frac{3}{4}}$ $\boxed{\frac{1}{3}}$ $\boxed{\frac{10}{30}}$ $\boxed{\frac{6}{15}}$ $\boxed{\frac{12}{16}}$ $\boxed{\frac{4}{10}}$ $\boxed{\frac{2}{5}}$ $\boxed{\frac{6}{8}}$ $\boxed{\frac{4}{12}}$

Key points

- When you add or subtract fractions with the same denominator, add or subtract the numerators. Then write the result over the same denominator.
- To work out a fraction of a quantity, divide the quantity by the denominator and then multiply by the numerator.

△ Purposeful practice 1

1 Work out

a $\frac{1}{3} + \frac{1}{3}$ b $\frac{2}{3} - \frac{1}{3}$ c $\frac{1}{5} + \frac{2}{5}$ d $\frac{3}{5} - \frac{1}{5}$ e $\frac{2}{5} + \frac{2}{5}$

f $\frac{4}{5} - \frac{2}{5}$ g $\frac{3}{5} + \frac{1}{5}$ h $\frac{4}{5} - \frac{1}{5}$ i $\frac{4}{5} - \frac{3}{5}$ j $\frac{1}{7} + \frac{3}{7}$

k $\frac{4}{7} - \frac{3}{7}$ l $\frac{4}{7} - \frac{1}{7}$ m $\frac{4}{7} + \frac{2}{7}$ n $\frac{6}{7} - \frac{4}{7}$ o $\frac{6}{7} - \frac{3}{7}$

2 Giving your answers in their simplest form, work out

a $\frac{1}{4} + \frac{1}{4}$ b $\frac{3}{4} - \frac{1}{4}$ c $\frac{1}{6} + \frac{1}{6}$ d $\frac{5}{6} - \frac{1}{6}$ e $\frac{1}{8} + \frac{1}{8}$

f $\frac{1}{8} + \frac{3}{8}$ g $\frac{3}{8} + \frac{3}{8}$ h $\frac{7}{8} - \frac{5}{8}$ i $\frac{7}{8} - \frac{3}{8}$ j $\frac{7}{8} - \frac{1}{8}$

k $\frac{1}{9} + \frac{2}{9}$ l $\frac{1}{9} + \frac{5}{9}$ m $\frac{2}{9} + \frac{4}{9}$ n $\frac{4}{9} - \frac{1}{9}$ o $\frac{8}{9} - \frac{2}{9}$

Reflect and reason

Lin adds $\frac{2}{5}$ and $\frac{1}{5}$ like this: $\frac{2}{5} + \frac{1}{5} = \frac{2+1}{5+5} = \frac{3}{10}$

Explain what Lin has done wrong.

△ Purposeful practice 2

1 Find the missing numbers.

a $\frac{1}{3} + \frac{\square}{3} = 1$ b $\frac{2}{3} + \frac{\square}{3} = 1$ c $\frac{1}{4} + \frac{\square}{4} = 1$ d $\frac{1}{5} + \frac{\square}{5} = 1$ e $\frac{1}{6} + \frac{\square}{6} = 1$

2 Work out

a $1 - \frac{1}{3}$ b $1 - \frac{2}{3}$ c $1 - \frac{3}{4}$ d $1 - \frac{3}{5}$

e $1 - \frac{5}{6}$ f $1 - \frac{5}{7}$ g $1 - \frac{5}{8}$ h $1 - \frac{5}{9}$

Reflect and reason

Sam subtracts $\frac{3}{4}$ from 1 like this: $1 - \frac{3}{4} = \frac{1-3}{4} = \frac{-2}{4}$

Explain what Sam has done wrong.

1 Work out

a $\frac{1}{2}$ of 6   **b** $\frac{1}{3}$ of 12   **c** $\frac{1}{4}$ of 12   **d** $\frac{1}{5}$ of 30

e $\frac{1}{6}$ of 30   **f** $\frac{1}{7}$ of 14   **g** $\frac{1}{8}$ of 16   **h** $\frac{1}{9}$ of 18

2 Work out

a $\frac{2}{3}$ of 12   **b** $\frac{2}{5}$ of 30   **c** $\frac{2}{7}$ of 14   **d** $\frac{2}{9}$ of 18   **e** $\frac{3}{4}$ of 12

f $\frac{3}{5}$ of 30   **g** $\frac{3}{7}$ of 14   **h** $\frac{3}{8}$ of 16   **i** $\frac{4}{5}$ of 30   **j** $\frac{4}{7}$ of 14

Reflect and reason

Sara and Lee work out $\frac{4}{5}$ of £15.
Explain why they are both correct.
Which is the better method and why?

Sara	Lee
$15 \div 5 = 3$	$15 \div 5 = 3$
$4 \times 3 = 12$	$3 + 3 + 3 + 3 = 12$

⊠ **Problem-solving practice**

1 Look at the diagram.
Nia says that $\frac{1}{2}$ of the diagram is shaded.
Nia is right. Explain why.

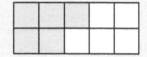

2 Jack is asked to work out $\frac{4}{5} - \frac{3}{5}$
Jack writes
$\frac{4}{5} - \frac{3}{5} = \frac{4-3}{5-5} = \frac{1}{0}$
Jack is incorrect.

  a Explain Jack's mistake.

  b Write the correct answer.

3 Alex asked some students their favourite sport.
The table shows Alex's results.
Alex says, '$\frac{1}{4}$ of the students prefer netball.'

Sport	swimming	netball	football	tennis
Number of students	5	30	50	15

Alex is incorrect. Explain why.

4 Aisha has 60 sweets.
$\frac{1}{3}$ of the sweets are red and $\frac{1}{4}$ of the sweets are yellow.
How many sweets are not red or yellow? You must show your working.

5 Rahul and Felix work in a restaurant.
They share the tips depending on how long they each worked.
This month they received £80 in tips.
Rahul gets $\frac{7}{10}$ of the tips and Felix gets the rest.
How much money does Felix get? You must show your working.

Key points

- You can convert a decimal to a fraction by looking at the place value.
- You can convert a fraction to a decimal by writing an equivalent fraction with a denominator of 10 or 100 and then using place value.

Purposeful practice 1

1 Convert each decimal to a fraction in its simplest form.

   a 0.1   **b** 0.2   **c** 0.3   **d** 0.4   **e** 0.5

   f 0.6   **g** 0.7   **h** 0.8   **i** 0.9

2 Convert each fraction to a decimal.

   a $\dfrac{1}{5}$ **b** $\dfrac{2}{5}$ **c** $\dfrac{3}{5}$ **d** $\dfrac{4}{5}$

3 Convert each decimal to a fraction in its simplest form.

   a 0.01   **b** 0.02   **c** 0.03   **d** 0.04   **e** 0.05

   f 0.06   **g** 0.07   **h** 0.08   **i** 0.09

4 Convert each fraction to a decimal.

   a $\dfrac{1}{100}$ **b** $\dfrac{3}{100}$ **c** $\dfrac{7}{100}$ **d** $\dfrac{9}{100}$ **e** $\dfrac{1}{50}$

   f $\dfrac{3}{50}$ **g** $\dfrac{1}{25}$ **h** $\dfrac{2}{25}$ **i** $\dfrac{1}{20}$

Reflect and reason

Tracy writes $0.03 = \dfrac{3}{10}$

What mistake has Tracy made?

Purposeful practice 2

1 Convert each decimal to a fraction in its simplest form.

   a 0.12   **b** 0.15   **c** 0.23   **d** 0.25   **e** 0.33   **f** 0.36

   g 0.42   **h** 0.56   **i** 0.65   **j** 0.72   **k** 0.81   **l** 0.92

2 Convert each fraction to a decimal.

   a $\dfrac{6}{50}$ **b** $\dfrac{12}{50}$ **c** $\dfrac{3}{20}$ **d** $\dfrac{6}{20}$ **e** $\dfrac{12}{20}$ **f** $\dfrac{9}{25}$

   g $\dfrac{18}{25}$ **h** $\dfrac{21}{50}$ **i** $\dfrac{42}{50}$ **j** $\dfrac{14}{25}$ **k** $\dfrac{7}{25}$

Reflect and reason

$0.04 = \dfrac{1}{25}$

How can you use this fact to work out decimal equivalents for these fractions?

$\dfrac{2}{25}$ $\dfrac{3}{25}$ $\dfrac{6}{25}$ $\dfrac{12}{25}$ $\dfrac{24}{25}$

⊠ Problem-solving practice

1 Eliza is asked to write $\frac{1}{2}$ as a decimal.
She writes

$$\frac{1}{2} = 1.2$$

Eliza is wrong. Explain why.

2 Copy and complete

$$\frac{13}{20} = \frac{\square}{100} = 0.\square\square$$

3 Match each pair of equivalent values.

| $\frac{3}{4}$ | $\frac{1}{2}$ | $\frac{1}{4}$ | $\frac{1}{5}$ | $\frac{7}{10}$ | $\frac{4}{5}$ |

| 0.2 | 0.5 | 0.7 | 0.75 | 0.8 | 0.25 |

4 Which is the smallest value out of 0.4, $\frac{3}{5}$ and $\frac{3}{10}$?
Explain why.

5 State whether each statement is true or false.
Give reasons for your answers.

a $\frac{2}{5} = 2.5$ **b** $\frac{3}{20} = 0.3$ **c** $\frac{9}{25} = 0.36$

6 Zara has a bag of red, orange and yellow sweets.
23 of the sweets are red.
17 of the sweets are orange.
10 of the sweets are yellow.

a What fraction of the sweets are orange or yellow?

b Write your answer to part **a** as a decimal.

7 A survey is done to find out how a group of students travel to school.
The table shows the results.

Transport	walk	car	bus	cycle
Number of students	6	8	4	7

Write the number of these students that cycle to school as a decimal.

8 During an athletics competition a team won

14 gold medals

7 silver medals

4 bronze medals

Maddy correctly writes the fraction of the gold medals as $\frac{14}{25}$

She then writes $\frac{14}{25} = 0.14$

Maddy is incorrect. Explain why.

Key points

- Per cent, or percent, means 'out of 100'. % stands for 'per cent'.
  50% means '50 out of 100', which is $\frac{50}{100}$
- You can write any percentage as a fraction with denominator 100.
- You can write a percentage as a fraction and then convert to a decimal.
- You can write a decimal as a fraction with denominator 100 and then convert to a percentage.

△ Purposeful practice 1

1 Convert each fraction to a percentage.

a $\frac{29}{100}$ **b** $\frac{52}{100}$ **c** $\frac{79}{100}$ **d** $\frac{99}{100}$

e $\frac{30}{100}$ **f** $\frac{3}{100}$ **g** $\frac{80}{100}$ **h** $\frac{8}{100}$

2 Convert each fraction to

   i a fraction with denominator 100   **ii** a percentage

a $\frac{1}{10}$ **b** $\frac{3}{10}$ **c** $\frac{7}{10}$ **d** $\frac{9}{10}$ **e** $\frac{1}{50}$

f $\frac{9}{50}$ **g** $\frac{13}{50}$ **h** $\frac{23}{50}$ **i** $\frac{36}{50}$ **j** $\frac{41}{50}$

k $\frac{49}{50}$ **l** $\frac{1}{25}$ **m** $\frac{7}{25}$ **n** $\frac{11}{25}$ **o** $\frac{15}{25}$

p $\frac{23}{25}$ **q** $\frac{1}{20}$ **r** $\frac{9}{20}$ **s** $\frac{13}{20}$ **t** $\frac{19}{20}$

3 Convert each fraction to

   i a decimal   **ii** a percentage

a $\frac{1}{10}$ **b** $\frac{3}{10}$ **c** $\frac{7}{10}$ **d** $\frac{9}{10}$

e $\frac{10}{10}$ **f** $\frac{1}{2}$ **g** $\frac{1}{4}$ **h** $\frac{3}{4}$

i $\frac{1}{5}$ **j** $\frac{2}{5}$ **k** $\frac{4}{5}$ **l** $\frac{5}{5}$

Reflect and reason

Write down the percentage/fraction equivalents you are fluent in. This means the ones you 'just know' without having to work them out.

△ Purposeful practice 2

1 Convert each percentage to a decimal.

   a 1%   **b** 6%   **c** 8%   **d** 10%   **e** 20%   **f** 60%

   g 80%   **h** 100%   **i** 18%   **j** 23%   **k** 42%   **l** 55%

   m 62%   **n** 74%   **o** 92%   **p** 105%   **q** 110%   **r** 120%

2 Convert each decimal to a percentage.

a 0.32	**b** 0.3	**c** 0.02	**d** 0.78	**e** 0.7	**f** 0.08
g 0.56	**h** 0.5	**i** 0.06	**j** 0.93	**k** 0.9	**l** 0.03
m 1.35	**n** 1.0	**o** 1.3	**p** 1.05		

Reflect and reason

Lucy says, '8% is equivalent to 0.8.'

Explain Lucy's mistake.

Problem-solving practice

1 Sanjay is asked to write $\frac{1}{5}$ as a percentage.

He writes $\frac{1}{5} = 5\%$

Is Sanjay correct? Explain why.

2 Which decimal is equivalent to $\frac{115}{100}$?

A 0.115 B 1.15 C 11.5 D 115.0

3 Match each pair of equivalent values.

$\frac{3}{4}$	$\frac{1}{2}$	$\frac{2}{5}$	$\frac{3}{10}$	$\frac{43}{50}$	$\frac{7}{20}$

30%	35%	86%	40%	75%	50%

4 Which is bigger, $\frac{1}{4}$ or 30%?

Give a reason for your answer.

5 Decide whether each statement is true or false.
Give reasons for your answers.

a $\frac{31}{50} = 62\%$

b $\frac{1}{20} = 20\%$

c $\frac{7}{10} = 7\%$

6 During a week, a vet treats dogs, cats and rabbits.
21 of the animals treated are dogs.
18 of the animals are cats.
11 of the animals are rabbits.

a What fraction of the animals are **not** dogs?

b Write your answer to part **a** as a percentage.

7 During a swimming gala, a team won
11 front crawl races
6 back stroke races
2 breast stroke races
1 butterfly race

What percentage of the wins were not front crawl races?

Key points

- 10% is the same as $\frac{1}{10}$. To find 10% of an amount, divide by 10.

  You can then use 10% to find other percentages.
- 50% is the same as $\frac{1}{2}$. To find 50% of an amount, divide by 2.
- You can use a multiplier to work out a percentage, by using the decimal equivalent of the percentage.

Purposeful practice 1

1 Copy and complete

   a $10\% \times 2 = \square\%$ **b** $10\% \times \square = 60\%$

   c $10\% \times \square = 30\%$ **d** $10\% \times \square = 40\%$

   e $10\% \times 9 = \square\%$ **f** $10\% \times \square = 70\%$

   g $10\% \div \square = 5\%$ **h** $10\% \div 10 = \square\%$

2 Work out

   a 10% of 60 cm   **b** 20% of 60 cm   **c** 60% of 60 cm

   d 50% of 60 cm   **e** 5% of 60 cm   **f** 1% of 60 cm

3 Work out

   a 10% of 12 kg   **b** 30% of 12 kg   **c** 70% of 12 kg

   d 50% of 12 kg   **e** 5% of 12 kg   **f** 1% of 12 kg

4 Work out

   a 10% of £42   **b** 20% of £42   **c** 40% of £42

   d 50% of £42   **e** 5% of £42   **f** 1% of £42

Reflect and reason

For **Q4a**, Melissa writes 10% of £42 is £4.2.
Explain the mistake she has made.

Purposeful practice 2

1 Work out

   a 10% of £300   **b** 1% of £300   **c** 11% of £300

   d 20% of £300   **e** 2% of £300   **f** 22% of £300

   g 5% of £300   **h** 7% of £300   **i** 27% of £300

2 Work out

   a 10% of £250   **b** 5% of £250   **c** 1% of £250

   d 15% of £250   **e** 6% of £250   **f** 16% of £250

   g 30% of £250   **h** 36% of £250   **i** 45% of £250

Reflect and reason

In **Q2**, how could you use the answers to earlier parts of the question to answer part **f**?
Write three more percentages of £250 that you could find using your answers to **Q2**.

1 Write these percentages as decimals.
   a 10%   **b** 20%   **c** 30%   **d** 40%   **e** 50%
   f 60%   **g** 70%   **h** 80%   **i** 90%   **j** 1%

2 Copy and complete
   a $0.2 \times 500\,g = \square\,g = \square\% \text{ of } 500\,g$
   b $0.5 \times 500\,g = \square\,g = \square\% \text{ of } 500\,g$
   c $0.7 \times 500\,g = \square\,g = \square\% \text{ of } 500\,g$
   d $0.9 \times 500\,g = \square\,g = \square\% \text{ of } 500\,g$

Reflect and reason

Which of these methods calculates 20% of an amount? Choose all options that apply.
A   Find 10% and double   B   Multiply by 20   C   Multiply by 0.2
D   Divide by 10 and double   E   Divide by 20   F   Divide by 5
G   Divide by 0.2

⊠ Problem-solving practice

1 Jeff works out 20% of 320.
  He writes
  20% of 320 = 320 ÷ 20 = 16
  Explain Jeff's mistake.

2 Megan earns £2200 per month.
  Megan saves 5% of her earnings and spends the rest.
     a How much does Megan save each month?
     b How much does Megan spend each month?

3 Which is greater, 65% of 80 or 45% of 120?
  You must show your working.

4 There are 800 students at a school.
  The school has a daily attendance target of 95%.
  On Friday, there were 756 students at school.
  Was this enough to meet the attendance target? Explain your answer.

5 On one day, a shop has 120 customers.
  85% of the customers pay with a card and the rest of the customers pay with cash.
  How many customers pay with cash? You must show your working.

6 Sunil wants to buy a jacket costing £60.
  He has two vouchers but he can only use
  one of them.

  | £8 off when you spend £50 or more | 15% off all clothing |

  Explain why Sunil should choose the 15% off voucher.

7 Jill earns £480 each week.
  She asks for a pay rise of £20 a week, but instead she is offered a 5% pay rise.
  Is the offer more than Jill asked for? You must show your working.

8 What is the difference between 42 minutes and 65% of an hour?
  Give your answer in minutes. You must show your working.

6 Probability

6.1 The language of probability

Key points

- In probability, an event is something that might happen.
- Probability is the chance that an event will happen. You can show probability on a probability scale.
- Even chance means that an event is as likely to happen as it is not.
- 'Likely' means an event has more than an even chance of happening, and 'unlikely' means it has less than an even chance.
- All probabilities have a value between 0 and 1.

⚠ Purposeful practice

1 You pick a counter from one of these bags without looking.

a From which bag(s) are you
  i likely to pick a blue counter
  iii certain to pick a white counter
  v unlikely to pick a white counter
  ii unlikely to pick a blue counter
  iv likely to pick a white counter
  vi unlikely to pick a red counter?

b Which bag gives an even chance of picking a red counter?

c From which bag(s) is it impossible to pick a
  i blue counter   **ii** red counter   **iii** white counter?

2 Copy the probability scale and mark on it the likelihood for each spinner to land on blue.

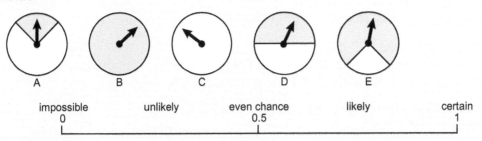

3 The probability scale shows the probabilities of events P, Q, R, S, T, U, V, W.

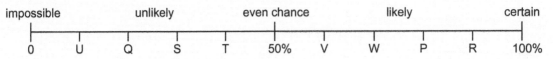

a Which events are
  i unlikely   **ii** likely?

b Write the probability of each event as a percentage. The first one is done for you.

Probability of U = 10%

Reflect and reason

Cara says, 'Event P and event R are both likely. This must mean they have the same probability.'

Is Cara correct? Explain your answer.

What is the advantage of using numbers to describe probabilities?

⊠ Problem-solving practice

1 Look at these bags of counters and the probability words.
Match the probability of picking a red counter from each bag with the correct word(s).

| impossible | unlikely | even chance | likely | certain |

2 Look at these sets of blue (B), white (W) and red (R) counters.

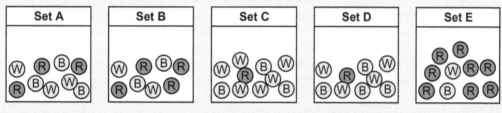

a From which set of counters are you unlikely to pick a red?

b From which set are you likely to pick a white?

Sienna says, 'There is an even chance of picking a blue counter from set A and set B.'

c Explain why Sienna is wrong.

d Draw a set of counters where there is an even chance of picking a blue counter.

3 The probability of an event is shown by the cross on the probability scale.

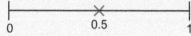

Write down a possible event for this probability.

4 Here is an 8-sided spinner.
The letters A, B, C and D are used to represent each section.
Each letter can be used more than once.
The probability that the spinner will land on D is likely.
The probability that the spinner will land on any of the other letters is unlikely.
Copy the spinner and write a letter in each section so that it matches this description.

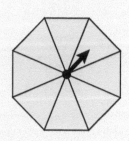

Key points

- Picking an item at random means each item has the same chance of being picked.
- Outcomes are the possible results of an event. The possible outcomes of flipping a coin are 'heads' and 'tails'.
- Probability of an event happening = $\dfrac{\text{number of successful outcomes}}{\text{total number of possible outcomes}}$
- P(X) means the probability that X happens.

Purposeful practice 1

A card is picked at random.

1 Work out the probability of picking an even number from each set.

   a 1 2   **b** 1 3   **c** 2 4   **d** 1 2 3   **e** 1 2 4

   f 1 3 5   **g** 2 4 6   **h** 1 2 3 4   **i** 1 2 4 6   **j** 1 2 3 5

2 Work out the probability of picking a red (R) card from each set.

   a R B   **b** B B   **c** R R   **d** R B B   **e** R R B

   f R R R   **g** B B B   **h** R B R B   **i** B R R R   **j** B R B B

Reflect and reason

Why do **Q1i** and **Q2i** have the same answer?

Explain using the number of possible outcomes and number of successful outcomes.

Purposeful practice 2

A counter is picked from a bag of counters at random.

For each bag, copy and complete: P(red) = ☐   P(blue) = ☐

1 a   **b**   **c**

   d   **e**   **f**

2 a   **b**   **c**   **d**   **e**

Reflect and reason

In which question were the probabilities for red and blue the same? Explain why.

Dom says, 'Each bag has only 2 colours of counters: red or blue. So the probability of picking red must be $\frac{1}{2}$.' Use your answers to **Q1** and **Q2** to explain why Dom is wrong.

⊠ Problem-solving practice

1 Look at these number cards.

1 2 2 3 3 3 4 4 4

A card is chosen at random.
Work out the probability that the card shows the number

a 1

b 2

c 3

Amber says, 'The probability of choosing a card with an even number on it is $\frac{1}{2}$ because there are two types of numbers: odd and even.'

d Is Amber correct? Explain your answer.

e What is the probability that the card shows an even number?

2 Look at this 7-sided spinner.

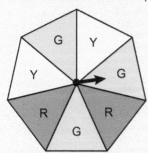

Which colours do you have an equal chance of landing on?
Write the probabilities as fractions to help you explain why.

3 Look at these spinners and probabilities.

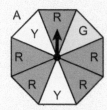 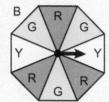  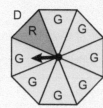 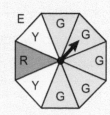

$P(G) = \frac{7}{8}$ $P(G) = \frac{1}{4}$ $P(G) = \frac{1}{8}$ $P(G) = \frac{5}{8}$ $P(G) = \frac{1}{2}$ $P(G) = \frac{3}{8}$

a Match each spinner with the probability that it lands on green (G).
(One probability won't be used.)

b Draw and label an 8-sided spinner for the probability you did not use.

4 There are 7 milk, 3 white and 2 dark chocolates in a box.
One of the chocolates is chosen at random.
Write down the probability that it is a milk chocolate.

5 There are 32 children in a class.
15 of the children have blue eyes.
One of the children is chosen at random.
Write down the probability that the chosen child does **not** have blue eyes.

Key points

- P(green or blue) means the probability of green or blue.
- P(event not happening) = 1 − P(event happening)

△ Purposeful practice 1

Here is a set of red (R), white (W) and yellow (Y) counters.

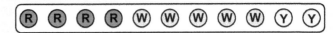

Work out

1	P(R)	**2**	P(not R)	**3**	P(W)
4	P(not W)	**5**	P(Y)	**6**	P(not Y)
7	P(R or W)	**8**	P(not R or W)	**9**	P(R or Y)
10	P(not R or Y)	**11**	P(W or Y)	**12**	P(not W or Y)

Reflect and reason

Using the counters in Purposeful practice 1, work out P(R or Y or W).

Copy and complete this sentence: P(R or Y or W) = ☐ because it is _____ that you will pick red or yellow or white.

Next, work out P(not R or Y or W).

Copy and complete this sentence: P(not R or Y or W) = ☐ because it is _____ to pick a counter that is not red or yellow or white.

△ Purposeful practice 2

The probability scale shows the probabilities of events A to E.

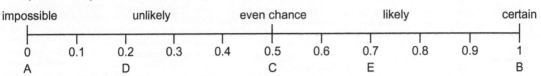

Write the probability of each event in numbers and words. The first one is done for you.

1 P(A) = 0, impossible

2	P(B)	**3**	P(C)	**4**	P(D)
5	P(E)	**6**	P(not A)	**7**	P(not B)
8	P(not C)	**9**	P(not D)	**10**	P(not E)

Reflect and reason

Use appropriate words to complete these sentences.

When the probability of an event is zero, the probability that it does not happen is _____.

When an event is likely to happen, the probability that it does not happen is _____.

△ Purposeful practice 3

A counter is picked from this bag at random.

Work out

1 P(G)	**2** P(R)	**3** P(W)
4 P(not W)	**5** P(R or W)	**6** P(not R or W)
7 P(R or W or B)	**8** P(not G)	**9** P(W or B or G)
10 P(not R)	**11** P(not R or W or B)	**12** P(G or R)

Reflect and reason

Explain why the answers to **Q7** and **Q8** are the same.

In what two ways could you work out P(R or B or G)?

⊠ Problem-solving practice

1 The probability of a bus being late is 0.3
   What is the probability that bus will not be late?

2 A weather forecast says, 'There is a 65% chance that it will rain tomorrow.'
   Amil says, 'That means the chance that it won't rain tomorrow is 35%.'
   Is Amil correct? Explain your answer.

3 A bag contains some coloured counters.
   The probability of picking a red counter is $\frac{3}{8}$
   What is the probability of not picking a red counter?

4 Sadie has a bag of 25 coloured sweets.
   11 of the sweets are red, 8 are green and the rest are yellow.
   Write the probability that Sadie

   a takes a yellow sweet

   b does not take a green sweet

   c takes a blue sweet

5 Match each probability with the correct spinner.

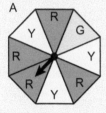 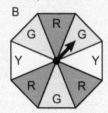 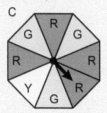 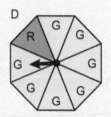 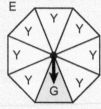

$P(\text{not R}) = \frac{5}{8}$	$P(\text{G or R}) = \frac{7}{8}$	$P(\text{not Y}) = \frac{1}{8}$	$P(\text{R or G}) = \frac{5}{8}$	$P(\text{R or G}) = 1$

6 Use these cards to make a set of five cards so that $P(\text{not 1}) = \frac{3}{5}$ and $P(4) = \frac{1}{5}$.

   ⎡1⎤⎡2⎤⎡3⎤⎡4⎤⎡5⎤

   You may use each number card more than once.

Key points

- You can use the results of an experiment to estimate probabilities.
  This is called experimental probability.
- Experimental probability $= \dfrac{\text{frequency of event}}{\text{total frequency}}$

⚠ Purposeful practice 1

Work out the experimental probabilities for each outcome.
Give your answers as fractions.

1 A coin is flipped.

Result	Frequency	Experimental probability
head	56	
tail	44	
Total		

2 A dice is rolled.

Result	Frequency	Experimental probability
6	16	
not 6		
Total	150	

3 A train arrives.

Train arrives	Frequency	Experimental probability
on time	147	
late		
Total	200	

4 Judy arrives at school.

Judy arrives	Frequency	Experimental probability
early		
on time	15	
late	5	
Total	21	

Reflect and reason

Deb says, 'In **Q1** and **Q2**, rolling a dice and flipping a coin are experiments, but in **Q3** and **Q4**, trains and people arriving are not experiments. So you cannot calculate experimental probability for **Q3** and **Q4**.'
Explain why Deb is wrong.

⚠ Purposeful practice 2

Leo and his friends roll the same dice a number of times, and record the number of sixes they roll. Copy the table and use it to answer the questions.

Name	Number of rolls	Number of sixes	Experimental probability
Leo	1	0	
Vinny	19	7	
Maya	30	4	
Deepak	40	11	
Jess	30	8	

1 Work out the experimental probability of rolling a six for each set of results. Complete the last column of the table.

2 Work out the total number of
a sixes
b rolls

3 Use the total number of sixes and the total numbers of rolls to estimate the probability of rolling a six on this dice.

4 Explain why Leo cannot draw any conclusions from only one roll of a dice.

Reflect and reason

Which person's results give the best estimate for the probability of rolling a six with this dice? Why do you think that is?

☒ Problem-solving practice

1 A football manager records the number of times their team wins, loses or draws a match. The table shows the results.

Result	Frequency
win	3
lose	2
draw	2

a Use the manager's results to estimate the probability of the team winning or drawing their next match.

b How could the manager improve the accuracy of their estimate?

2 Sonia spins this spinner 50 times.
Her results are shown in the table.

Colour	Frequency
red	16
white	34

a Sonia says, 'The experimental probability of the spinner landing on red is $\frac{16}{34}$.' Is she correct? Explain why.

b Sonia says, 'The experimental probability of the spinner landing on white is $\frac{17}{25}$.' Is she correct? Explain your answer.

3 Jackson rolls a 4-sided dice.
He records his results in the table.

Result	Frequency
1	10
2	16
3	23
4	31

Jackson claims that the experimental probability of not rolling a 1 is $\frac{3}{4}$
Jackson is incorrect.
Is the experimental probability of not rolling a 1 greater than or less than $\frac{3}{4}$? Explain why.

Key point

- You can use probability to estimate expected number of times an outcome will occur.

△ Purposeful practice 1

In each question, a counter is picked at random from the bag.
Its colour is recorded and the counter is put back in the bag.

1 a Work out   **i**   P(red)   **ii**   P(blue)
   b A counter will be picked at random 10 times. Estimate the
      expected number of   **i**   red counters   **ii**   blue counters

2 a Work out
      i   P(red)   **ii**   P(blue)   **iii**   P(green)
   b A counter will be picked at random 20 times. Estimate the
      expected number of
      i   red counters   **ii**   blue counters   **iii**   green counters

3 a Work out
      i   P(red)   **ii**   P(blue)   **iii**   P(yellow)   **iv**   P(white)
   b A counter will be picked at random 30 times. Estimate the
      expected number of
      i   red counters   **ii**   blue counters
      iii   yellow counters   **iv**   white counters

4 a Work out
      i   P(red)   **ii**   P(blue)   **iii**   P(yellow)   **iv**   P(white)
   b A counter will be picked at random 30 times. Estimate the
      expected number of
      i   red counters   **ii**   blue counters
      iii   yellow counters   **iv**   white counters

Reflect and reason

Use the words 'lower' or 'higher' to complete these sentences about **Q3** and **Q4**.

The lower the probability of red, the _____ the expected number of red counters picked.

The higher the probability of red, the _____ the expected number of red counters picked.

△ Purposeful practice 2

1 For each spinner, estimate the expected number of times it will land on 'Win' in
   a   12 spins   **b**   24 spins

A   B   C   D   E   F

2 Each spinner in **Q1** costs £1 a spin.
You win £3 if it stops on 'Win'.
For each spinner, calculate the expected profit for 12 spins using the formula
Expected profit = expected winnings on 12 spins − cost of 12 spins.

3 Here are the results for 24 spins of this spinner.
First 12 spins: W L L W L L L W L L L L
Second 12 spins: L W L L W L L W W L L W

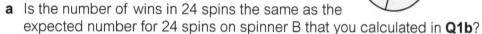

a Is the number of wins in 24 spins the same as the
expected number for 24 spins on spinner B that you calculated in **Q1b**?

b Is the number of wins in the first 12 spins the same as the expected number for
12 spins on spinner B that you calculated in **Q1b**?

c This spinner also costs £1 a spin and you win £3 if it stops on 'Win'.
Estimate your expected profit if you paid for these first 12 spins.

Reflect and reason

Emma says, 'My answers to **Q2** show I am unlikely to lose money with any of the
spinners, but I could actually win a lot!'

Use your answer to **Q3** to explain why Emma could lose money on the spinners.

⊠ Problem-solving practice

1 The probability of winning a game is $\frac{3}{4}$
Fay plays the game 20 times.
How many times should Fay expect to win the game?

2 Syed is going to choose a counter, without looking, from a bag
containing these red, blue and yellow counters.
He will then record the colour and put the counter back.
Syed will do this 150 times.
How many times should Syed expect to pick

a a red counter

b a blue counter?

Syed says, 'I expect to get 50 yellow counters because there are 3 colours and $\frac{1}{3}$ of
150 is 50.'

c Is Syed correct? Explain why.

3 Look at the spinners.

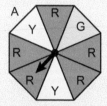 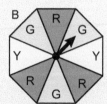 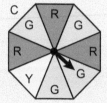 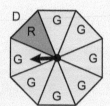 

Each spinner is spun 200 times.
For each expected outcome, say which spinner it is for.

a 125 yellow   **b** 100 green   **c** 125 red   **d** 75 green   **e** 175 green

7 Ratio and proportion

7.1 Direct proportion

Key points

- When two quantities are in direct proportion, as one increases or decreases, the other increases or decreases at the same rate. This means that when one quantity is zero, so is the other; when one is multiplied by 2, so is the other, and so on.
- In the unitary method, you find the value of one item before finding the value of more.

△ Purposeful practice 1

1 It costs £35 for 7 children to go swimming. How much does it cost for
  a 1 child   **b** 2 children   **c** 4 children
  d 6 children   **e** 12 children   **f** 24 children?

2 3 identical pen pots hold a total of 18 crayons. How many crayons fit in
  a 2 pen pots   **b** 4 pen pots   **c** 6 pen pots
  d 10 pen pots   **e** 16 pen pots   **f** 20 pen pots?

Reflect and reason

How can you use your answers to **Q1b** and **Q1c** to work out the answer to **Q1d**?
How can you use your answer to **Q1d** to work out the answers to **Q1f**?

△ Purposeful practice 2

A recipe for 6 people requires 3 teaspoons of curry powder.
How many teaspoons of curry powder are required for
1 1 person   **2** 3 people   **3** 12 people   **4** 4 people
5 7 people   **6** 11 people   **7** 22 people   **8** 25 people?

Reflect and reason

Sarah works out the answer to **Q1**.   1 person requires 6 ÷ 3 = 2 teaspoons
What mistake has Sarah made?

△ Purposeful practice 3

It costs £10 for 6 glow sticks. How much does it cost for
1 3 glow sticks   **2** 9 glow sticks   **3** 12 glow sticks
4 15 glow sticks   **5** 18 glow sticks   **6** 21 glow sticks?

Reflect and reason

For **Q1**, Kamal first works out $6 \overline{)10.\!^40^40^40}$ then he writes
$$\begin{array}{r} 1.666 \\ \times \quad\;\; 3 \\ \hline \end{array}$$
What is an easier method for Kamal to use?

Problem-solving practice

1 A recipe for 10 people uses 225 g of flour.
Jamie has 430 g of flour.
Does Jamie have enough flour for 20 people?
Give reasons for your answer.

2 It costs £35 for 5 people to go to the cinema.
Helen writes

The cost for 3 people = 3 × 5 = £15

Helen is incorrect.

a Explain what Helen may have done wrong.

b How much does it cost for 3 people?
You must show your working.

3 Emma changes some pounds into Euros for her holiday.
The exchange rate is £9 for €10.
Emma draws a table to help work out some prices.

Pounds (£)	Euros (€)
9	10
18	
45	
90	

a Copy and complete Emma's table.

b Emma buys a jacket costing €80.
Work out how much the jacket costs in pounds.
You can use your table to help you.

4 A car travels 450 miles using 50 litres of fuel.
There are 6 litres of fuel left in the tank.
Is this enough to travel 55 miles?
You must show your working.

5 A teacher buys 27 pens for her class.
The total cost of the pens is £40.50
Three new students join the class so she buys three more pens.
How much has the teacher spent on pens in total?

6 These ingredients make 10 shortbread biscuits.

> 150 g butter
> 75 g caster sugar
> 225 g flour

Dan has
   400 g butter
   200 g caster sugar
   500 g flour

Dan wants to make 30 shortbread biscuits.
He does not have enough of all the ingredients.
Work out how much more of each ingredient he needs.

Key points

- A ratio is a way of comparing two or more quantities. Ratios are written as numbers separated by a colon.
  For example, in this tile pattern there are 2 blue tiles and 1 red tile.

  The ratio of blue to red tiles is therefore 2 : 1.
- You can make the numbers in a ratio as small as possible by simplifying. You simplify a ratio by dividing the numbers in the ratio by the highest common factor.

Purposeful practice 1

1 Write the ratio of white tiles to green tiles for each image.

2 Draw white and grey tiles to show these ratios.

  a white to grey 3 : 2   **b** grey to white 3 : 2

  c grey to white 2 : 3   **d** white to grey 2 : 3

3 Draw white, grey and black tiles to show these ratios.

  a white to grey to black 1 : 2 : 2   **b** grey to white to black 1 : 2 : 2

  c white to black to grey 2 : 2 : 1   **d** black to grey to white 2 : 2 : 1

Reflect and reason

Which of your answers to **Q1** are the same ratio? Explain why.

Which of your answers to **Q2** are the same set of tiles? Explain why.

Which of your answers to **Q3** are the same set of tiles? Explain why.

Purposeful practice 2

Write each ratio in its simplest form.

1 a 10 : 15   **b** 4 : 6   **c** 10 : 6   **d** 4 : 10   **e** 12 : 8

   f 15 : 9   **g** 8 : 20   **h** 15 : 6   **i** 18 : 12   **j** 25 : 10

2 a 2 : 4 : 4   **b** 2 : 4 : 6   **c** 2 : 4 : 8   **d** 4 : 4 : 8

   e 2 : 2 : 4   **f** 4 : 6 : 8   **g** 2 : 4 : 2   **h** 4 : 8 : 4

Reflect and reason

Lucy says, '**Q1d**, **Q1g**, **Q1h** and **Q1j** all simplify to the same ratio, as all the answers give a ratio that includes the numbers 2 and 5.'

Is Lucy correct? Explain your answer.

1 Tariq is asked to simplify the ratio 6 : 12.
Tariq writes

6 : 12 simplifies to 2 : 1

Explain what Tariq has done wrong.

2 Sophie is asked to simplify the ratio 9 : 24.
She writes

9 : 24 simplifies to 4.5 : 12

Explain what Sophie has done wrong.

3 Shade a copy of this bar to show the colours black to white in the ratio 1 : 3.

4 Show that the ratio 15 : 20 : 30 simplifies to 3 : 4 : 6.

5 Match each ratio with its simplified ratio.

12 : 18	30 : 20	28 : 21	9 : 12	25 : 35	56 : 40
3 : 4	7 : 5	3 : 2	5 : 7	4 : 3	2 : 3

6 Copy and complete each statement.
  a 10 : ☐ simplifies to 5 : 7   **b** ☐ : 30 simplifies to 1 : 6
  c 42 : ☐ simplifies to 6 : 7   **d** ☐ : 60 simplifies to 2 : 5
  e 36 : ☐ : 20 simplifies to 9 : 7 : 5   **f** ☐ : 45 : 36 simplifies to 3 : 5 : 4

7 Nursery schools should have an adult-to-child ratio of 1 : 8.
If a nursery has 7 staff, how many children can they have?

8 On a school trip, the recommended ratio of staff to students is 1 : 12.
On a trip, there are 15 staff and 175 students.
Are there enough staff on the school trip?
Explain your answer.

9 Nicola has a necklace with red and white beads in the ratio 9 : 4.
Nicola says, 'My necklace has more than double the amount of red beads than white beads.'
Is Nicola correct? Explain your answer.

10 Stuart simplifies the ratio 36 : 42 : 60.
Stuart writes

$$\div 12 \left(\overset{36 \, : \, 42 \, : \, 60}{\underset{3 \, : \, 7 \, : \, 5}{\div 6}} \right) \div 12$$

Stuart is incorrect.
  a What is Stuart's mistake?
  b Simplify the ratio 36 : 42 : 60.
  c Write a ratio that does simplify to 3 : 7 : 5.

Key points

- Multiplying all the numbers in a ratio by the same number gives an equivalent ratio.
- In some ratio problems, you are given the ratio and one part, and asked to find the other part. In other ratio problems, you are given the ratio and total and asked to find the parts.

△ Purposeful practice 1

1 Which of these ratios are equivalent?

A 2 : 8	B 2 : 12	C 12 : 4	D 8 : 4
E 4 : 1	F 18 : 6	G 3 : 18	H 24 : 12
I 3 : 12	J 1 : 6	K 1 : 4	

2 A gardener always plants snowdrops to daffodil bulbs in the ratio 7 : 2.
   a How many snowdrop bulbs does she plant in a garden where she plants
      i   2 daffodil bulbs   ii 4 daffodil bulbs
      iii 14 daffodil bulbs   iv 50 daffodil bulbs?
   b How many daffodil bulbs does she plant in a garden where she plants
      i   7 snowdrop bulbs   ii 21 snowdrop bulbs
      iii 42 snowdrop bulbs   iv 140 snowdrop bulbs?

Reflect and reason

Why does the gardener in **Q2** never plant an odd number of daffodil bulbs?

△ Purposeful practice 2

1 A plastic tube is 12 cm long.
   The tube is to be cut into two smaller pieces.
   How long is each piece of the tube if it is cut in the ratio
   a 5 : 7   b 5 : 1   c 3 : 1   d 2 : 1?

2 Different lengths of ribbon are cut into different ratios.
   What lengths are the two pieces of ribbon when
   a 5 m is cut in the ratio 2 : 3   b 10 m is cut in the ratio 2 : 3
   c 15 m is cut in the ratio 2 : 3   d 20 m is cut in the ratio 2 : 3
   e 6 m is cut in the ratio 1 : 2   f 12 m is cut in the ratio 1 : 2
   g 8 m is cut in the ratio 1 : 3   h 16 m is cut in the ratio 1 : 3?

Reflect and reason

Sam says, 'I can use the answers to **Q2** parts **a–d** to predict the two lengths when 35 m is cut in the ratio 2 : 3, without having to do a calculation.'
Explain the pattern Sam has noticed.
What is 35 m cut in the ratio 2 : 3?

1 Dominic is asked to write a ratio that is equivalent to 4 : 3.
Dominic writes
16 : 12
Is Dominic correct? Explain your answer.

2 Write three ratios that are equivalent to the ratio 1 : 4.

3 Put these ratios into three groups of equivalent ratios.

4 : 5	3 : 5	21 : 35	60 : 70	27 : 45	12 : 20
6 : 7	12 : 15	44 : 55	30 : 35	32 : 40	12 : 14

4 Evie is asked to find equivalent ratios using whole numbers only.

$$\times\Box\left(\begin{array}{c}2 : \Box \\ \Box : 9\end{array}\right)\times\Box$$

Evie fills in three of the boxes and then realises she is wrong:

$$\times 2\left(\begin{array}{c}2 : \Box \\ 4 : 9\end{array}\right)\times 2$$

  a How does Evie know she is wrong?
  b What possible answers could Evie have given?

5 Imani's recipe uses flour and butter in the ratio 5 : 2.
Imani uses a total mass of 350 g of the two ingredients.
What mass of each ingredient was used?

6 Abir and Tristan share £250 in the ratio 2 : 3.
How much more money does Tristan get than Abir?

7 Ava and Felix each have a piece of string and cut it.
Ava's string is 50 m long and she cuts it in the ratio 2 : 3.
Felix's string is 40 m long and he cuts it in the ratio 3 : 5.
After the string has been cut, who has
  a the longest piece of string?
     How long is this piece?
  b the shortest piece of string?
     How long is this piece?
What is the difference in length between
  c Ava's two pieces of string
  d Felix's two pieces of string?

8 Julie makes a drink by mixing orange juice and lemonade in the ratio 3 : 7.
Julie uses 150 ml of orange juice.
How much drink does she have altogether?

9 Doug mixes sand and cement in the ratio 3 : 1 to make concrete.
Doug has 150 kg of sand and 40 kg cement.
How much more cement does Doug need to use all of the sand?

Key points

- A ratio compares a part with another part.
- A proportion compares a part with a whole.
- You can write a proportion as a fraction, a decimal or a percentage.

△ Purposeful practice 1

1 What proportion of counters in each of these games are

  i red   **ii** blue?

Give your answers as fractions in their simplest form.

  a A game with 1 red counter and 2 blue counters

  b A game with 1 red counter and 3 blue counters

  c A game with 1 red counter and 4 blue counters

  d A game with 2 red counters and 3 blue counters

  e A game with 2 red counters and 4 blue counters

  f A game with 2 red counters and 6 blue counters

  g A game with 3 red counters and 6 blue counters

  h A game with 3 red counters and 9 blue counters

2 Write the ratio of red counters to blue counters for each game in **Q1**.
Write each ratio in its simplest form.

Reflect and reason

Look at your answers to **Q1a** and **Q2a**; **Q1b** and **Q2b**; **Q1c** and **Q2c**, and so on.

How can you use the proportions of red and blue counters to find the ratio of red to blue counters in a game? And how can you use the ratio to find the proportions?

△ Purposeful practice 2

The cinema has four showings of a movie on one day. Here are the number of adult and child tickets sold for the different showings.

	Adults	Children
11 am	15	35
2 pm	24	36
5 pm	66	54
8 pm	78	26

1 Work out the proportion of adults at each showing.
Give your answers as fractions in their simplest form.

2 Work out the proportion of children at each showing.
Give your answers as fractions in their simplest form.

3 Which showing had the greatest proportion of adults? Show your working.

4 Which showing had the greatest proportion of children? Show your working.

Reflect and reason

Here are Fred's answers to **Q1**. What mistakes has Fred made?

11 am $\frac{15}{35} = \frac{3}{7}$ 2 pm $\frac{24}{36} = \frac{2}{3}$ 5 pm $\frac{54}{66} = \frac{9}{11}$ 8 pm $\frac{26}{78} = \frac{13}{39}$

---

1 The ratio of boys to girls in a class is 5 : 4.

Clare says, '$\frac{4}{5}$ of the class are girls.'

Is Clare correct? Explain your answer.

2 The numbers of blue and red beads on some necklaces are given as ratios.
Copy and complete each of these, writing the number of blue and red beads as a fraction.

a $2 : 3 = \frac{2}{5}$ blue and $\frac{\square}{\square}$ red

b $5 : 1 = \frac{\square}{\square}$ blue and $\frac{1}{6}$ red

c $7 : 5 = \frac{\square}{\square}$ blue and $\frac{\square}{\square}$ red

d $2 : 7 = \frac{\square}{\square}$ blue and $\frac{\square}{\square}$ red

3 There are green and blue counters in some bags.
The fraction of green counters in each bag is given.
Copy and complete each of these, writing the ratio of green to blue counters.

a $\frac{1}{5} = \square : \square$ **b** $\frac{5}{7} = \square : \square$

c $\frac{11}{15} = \square : \square$ **d** $\frac{9}{40} = \square : \square$

4 In a fruit bowl, there are apples and oranges.

$\frac{5}{7}$ of the fruit are apples.

Write the ratio of apples to oranges in the fruit bowl.

5 Darren makes green paint by mixing blue and yellow paint in the ratio 2 : 10.
Jo makes green paint by mixing blue and yellow paint in the ratio 1 : 5.
Darker green paint has a higher proportion of blue paint.
Darren says, 'My paint is darker because $\frac{2}{10}$ is greater than $\frac{1}{5}$.'
Is Darren correct? Explain why.

6 Supermarket A sells food to other products in the ratio of 17 : 3.
Supermarket B sells food to other products in the ratio of 4 : 1.
Which supermarket sells the greater proportion of food?

7 The table shows the number of students who live within 3 miles of school at three different schools.

School	within 3 miles	outside 3 miles
A	180	70
B	370	130
C	720	280

Which school has the greatest proportion of students living within 3 miles?
You must show your working.

Key points

- To find a proportion as a percentage, first write the proportion as a fraction, then convert the fraction to a percentage.
- You can compare proportions using percentages.

△ Purposeful practice 1

1 Different boxes of chocolates contain different numbers of milk and dark chocolates. What proportion of chocolates in each of these boxes are

  i milk

  ii dark?

Write your answers as percentages.

  a Box 1: 7 milk and 3 dark

  b Box 2: 32 milk and 18 dark

  c Box 3: 12 milk and 13 dark

  d Box 4: 2 milk and 3 dark

  e Box 5: 12 milk and 8 dark

2 **a** Which box in **Q1** had the greatest proportion of milk chocolates?

  b Which box in **Q1** had the greatest proportion of dark chocolates?

Reflect and reason

Why was it easier to answer **Q2** with the proportions in **Q1** written as percentages rather than fractions?

△ Purposeful practice 2

Here are the ratios of students who are in a sports club to those who are not in a sports club for different Year 7 and Year 8 classes.

For each class, work out the proportion who are

a in a sports club

b not in a sports club

Write your answers as percentages.

1 Class 7A 1 : 9   2 Class 7B 3 : 7

3 Class 8D 19 : 31   4 Class 8C 9 : 16

5 Class 7C 1 : 3   6 Class 7D 2 : 3

7 Class 8A 3 : 17   8 Class 8B 7 : 13

Reflect and reason

How can you check your answers? (What should parts **a** and **b** add up to each time?)

Which class is most likely to be the most successful at sports day? Explain your answer.

Problem-solving practice

1 The ratio of Year 7 to Year 8 members at a sports club is 3 : 2.
Naomi says, '40% of the members are in Year 7.'
Toby says, '30% of the members are in Year 7.'
Wes says, '40% of the members are in Year 8.'
Who is correct? Explain why.

2 The percentages of red and yellow balls in a bag are given in pairs.
Match each pair of percentages with its correct ratio for red and yellow balls.

| 44% and 56% | | 40% and 60% | | 42% and 58% | | 48% and 52% |
| 21 : 29 | | 12 : 13 | | 11 : 14 | | 2 : 3 |

3 Some spinners are coloured blue and green.
Copy and complete to show the ratio and the percentage of each colour.
Where appropriate, give the ratio in its simplest form.

a ☐ : ☐ = 20% blue and 80% green   **b** ☐ : ☐ = 45% blue and 55% green
c ☐ : ☐ = 75% blue and ☐% green   **d** ☐ : ☐ = 36% blue and ☐% green

4 Flour makes up 35% of the mass of ingredients in a recipe.
Write the ratio of the mass of flour to the mass of other ingredients in its simplest form.

5 Ethan and Melissa are each given an identical shape.
Ethan colours his shape using red and green in the ratio 11 : 9.
Melissa colours her shape using red and green in the ratio 27 : 23.
Whose shape has the smaller proportion of red?
Use percentages to explain your answer.

6 Jay makes orange squash by mixing squash and water in the ratio 1 : 9.
Emily makes orange squash by mixing squash and water in the ratio 7 : 43.
Emily says, 'My orange squash is stronger because 7% of it is squash.'
Is Emily correct? Explain why.

7 A teacher sets a maths test on number and algebra topics.
Paper 1 has number and algebra questions in the ratio of 16 : 9.
Paper 2 has number and algebra questions in the ratio of 7 : 3.
Which paper has the greater proportion of number questions?
You must show your working.

8 The table shows the number of teachers
and total of all the staff at three different
primary schools.

a Which school has the greatest proportion
of teaching staff?
You must show your working.

School	Teachers	All staff
A	80	200
B	9	30
C	45	100

b Which school has the greatest proportion
of non-teaching staff?

9 Seb makes salt water by mixing 6 g of salt with 200 ml of water.
Ajay makes salt water by mixing 20 g of salt with 500 ml of water.
Who has the saltier water? Explain your answer.

Mixed exercises B

Mixed problem-solving practice B

1 Work out the difference between $\frac{3}{4}$ and 80%, giving your answer as a percentage.

2 Write these numbers in order of size. Start with the smallest number.
You must show your working.

0.2   30% $\frac{1}{4}$ 0.5 $\frac{2}{5}$

3 $2.8 \times 63 = 176.4$
Without calculating it, what is 2.8×6.3?

4 James buys 12 cans of cola. There are 330 ml of cola in each can.
Amelia buys 2 bottles of cola. There are 2 litres of cola in each bottle.
Amelia buys more cola than Jack. How much more does she buy?

5 Amy and Harry use a calculator to work out 10.234×46.59
Amy writes 476.80206
Harry writes 4768.0206
Work out an estimate to determine whose answer is correct.

6 Here is a petrol gauge in a car.
A full fuel tank in this car holds 50 litres of petrol.
Work out how much petrol is in the tank.

7 Esme plays a game.
She can win, lose or draw the game.
The probability that Esme will win the game is 0.4
The probability that Esme will lose the game is 0.15

a Work out the probability that she will draw the game.

Esme plays the game 120 times.

b Work out an estimate for the number of times she will win the game.

8 One day, a shop has 620 customers.
65% of the customers pay with a debit card.

$\frac{1}{5}$ of the customers pay with a credit card.

The rest pay with cash.
Work out how many customers pay with cash.

9 Work out the perimeter of this shape.

10 90% of this field is used to grow potatoes.
Work out the area of the field that is used to grow potatoes.

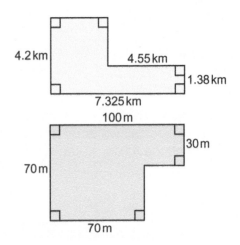

11 Arun bakes 240 cakes.
He bakes only vanilla, lemon and chocolate cakes.
35% of the cakes are vanilla cakes.
The ratio of the number of lemon cakes to the number of chocolate cakes is 5 : 7.
Work out the number of lemon cakes Arun bakes.

12 Sarah wants to cover a wall with tiles.
The wall measures 3 m by 5 m.
The tiles are squares with sides of length 20 cm.
The tiles are sold in packs, with 25 tiles in each pack.
Each pack of tiles costs £38
Sarah has £500
Can she buy enough packs of tiles to cover the wall?
Explain your answer.

13 There are 7 white beads and 13 red beads in a bag.
Toby takes a bead from the bag at random, looks at it and returns it to the bag.

a Write the probability that he takes a white bead.

Toby then adds 10 more beads, in a mix of red and white, to the bag.
The probability that he will take a white bead at random is now $\frac{2}{5}$

b Work out how many white beads and how many red beads Toby has added to the bag.

14 Mrs Walker recorded the number of Year 10 students and the number of Year 11 students absent from school each day last week.
The dual bar chart shows this information.

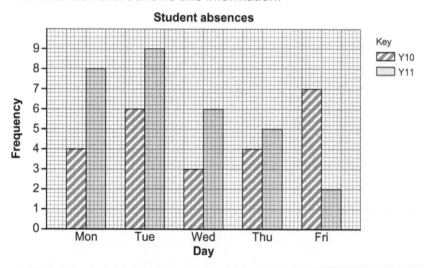

a Write the ratio of the number of Year 10 students to the number of Year 11 students absent from school last week. Give your answer in its simplest form.

b Mrs Walker says, 'Over $\frac{1}{2}$ of the total absences for Years 10 and 11 were on Monday and Tuesday.' Is she correct? Explain your answer.

c Work out, as a percentage, the proportion of the absences that were on Tuesday for each year group. What is the difference between the two proportions as a percentage?

8 Lines and angles

8.1 Measuring and drawing angles

Key points

- A whole turn is 360°.
- An acute angle is smaller than 90°.
- An obtuse angle is between 90° and 180°.
- A reflex angle is between 180° and 360°.

△ Purposeful practice 1

1 Work out the size of the angle that is not reflex in each sketch.

a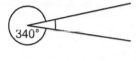

b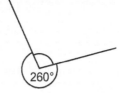

c

2 What angle less than 90° can you use to draw
   a 280°   b 300°   c 320°?

3 What angle between 90° and 180° can you use to draw
   a 220°   b 230°   c 250°?

Reflect and reason

Use 'acute' or 'obtuse' to complete these sentences.

An _____ angle has a reflex angle between 180° and 270°.

An _____ angle has a reflex angle between 270° and 360°.

△ Purposeful practice 2

1 i Describe each angle as 'acute', 'obtuse' or 'reflex'.

   ii Measure each angle.

a

b

c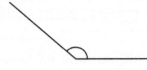

d

e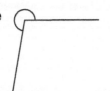

f

2 i Describe each angle as 'acute', 'obtuse' or 'reflex'.

ii Draw each angle.

a 20°   **b** 50°   **c** 70°   **d** 160°   **e** 130°

f 110°   **g** 200°   **h** 230°   **i** 250°

Reflect and reason

How does knowing the type of angle help you use a protractor to draw or measure it?

⊠ Problem-solving practice

1 Use a protractor to draw

    a a right angle   **b** an acute angle

    c an obtuse angle   **d** a reflex angle

    Label each angle with its measurement.

2 Eric measures this angle.
Eric says, 'The angle is 150 degrees.' He
is incorrect. What mistake has Eric made?

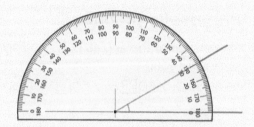

3 Ben measures angles a and b.
He writes
$a = 72°$ and $b = 281°$

    a Explain, without measuring, how you know Ben's
answers are not accurate enough.

    b Measure angles a and b.

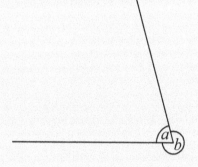

4 Measure the angle labelled x in the triangle.

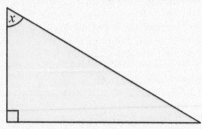

5 Vicki shades a circle so that it has four coloured
sections:
red (R), green (G), blue (B) and yellow (Y).
Show that Vicki used more green than any other colour.
Explain your answer using measurements of angles.

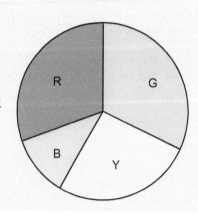

Key points

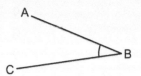

- This angle is called angle ABC or A$\hat{B}$C or ∠ABC.

- There are four types of triangle:

scalene

all angles and
sides different

isosceles

two equal angles
and sides

equilateral

all angles and
sides equal

right-angled

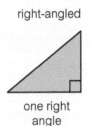

one right
angle

△ Purposeful practice 1

1 Name each of the angles D, E and F in two ways. The first one is
started for you.

Angle at D: ∠FD☐ or ∠ED☐

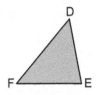

2 a Which six angles in the cloud match the angle shown here?

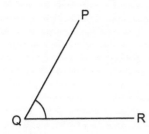

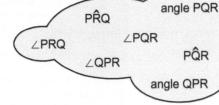

P$\hat{R}$Q   angle PQR   angle RQP

∠PRQ   ∠PQR   R$\hat{Q}$P   ∠RQP

∠QPR   P$\hat{Q}$R   angle PRQ

angle QPR

b What is the same about all the correct labels for this angle?

Reflect and reason

When you label an angle like this, is the order of the
letters important?

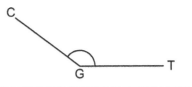

△ Purposeful practice 2

1 i Measure the angles of each triangle.

ii Name each type of triangle.

a

b

c

2 **i** Measure the angles of each triangle.
   ii Name each type of triangle.

a

b

c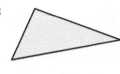

Reflect and reason

Is an equilateral triangle isosceles?

Can a right-angled triangle be isosceles or equilateral?

⊠ **Problem-solving practice**

1 Match each label to the correct angle.

   a ∠QPR   **b** ∠RQP   **c** ∠PRQ

A 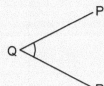   B 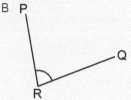   C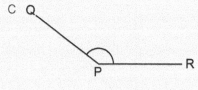

2 Copy and complete.
   ∠PQR = ∠□Q□

3 Chris measures the angles of triangle ABC. Chris writes
   ∠ABC = 80°, ∠BCA = 70° and ∠CAB = 30°

   Chris's numbers are right but his answer is incorrect.
   Explain how you can tell this without measuring the
   angles and write the correct answer.

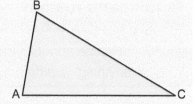

4 Name each type of triangle being described.
   a I have two equal sides and two equal angles.
   b All of my sides are different.
   c All of my sides and angles are equal.

5 Which of these triangles are isosceles? Explain why.

   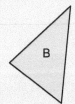   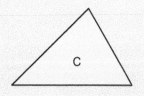   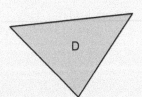

6 Rob says, 'This is an equilateral triangle.'
   Is Rob correct? Explain why.

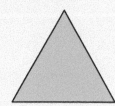

Key points

- You can use a ruler and protractor to draw a triangle accurately.
- 'Sketch' means draw a rough diagram. It does not have to be accurate.

△ Purposeful practice 1

Draw these triangles accurately.

1 a 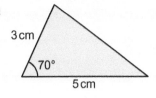   **b** 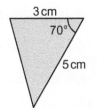   **c**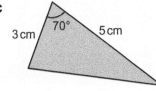

2 a 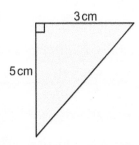   **b** 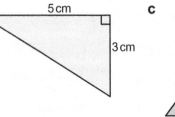   **c**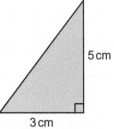

Reflect and reason

For each question in Purposeful practice 1,
what is the same about all three triangles?
What, if anything, is different about all three triangles?

△ Purposeful practice 2

1 Triangle PQR has ∠QRP = 40°, PR = 5 cm, RQ = 4 cm.
Which of these sketches is correct?

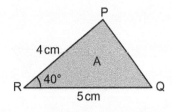   B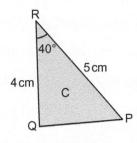

2 Triangle HJK has ∠KHJ = 110°, ∠JKH = 30°, KH = 4 cm.
Which of these sketches is correct?

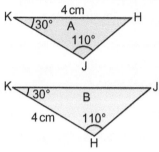

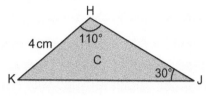

3 Draw the triangles described in **Q1** and **Q2** accurately. Use the sketches to help you.

Reflect and reason

Why is it helpful to draw and label a sketch before you draw a triangle accurately?

⬚ Problem-solving practice

1 a Match each description to its correct sketch.

  i Triangle PQR has ∠PQR = 50°, QR = 8 cm, PR = 6 cm

 ii Triangle PQR has ∠PRQ = 50°, PR = 8 cm, PQ = 6 cm

iii Triangle PQR has ∠PQR = 50°, PQ = 8 cm, PR = 6 cm

 iv Triangle PQR has ∠RPQ = 50°, PR = 8 cm, QR = 6 cm

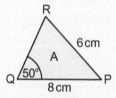
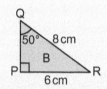
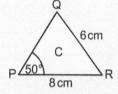
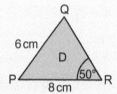

  b Use a ruler and protractor to draw each triangle accurately.

2 Oliver draws the triangle XYZ and writes

  ∠YXZ = 25° and XZ = 11.2 cm

Make an accurate drawing of the triangle XYZ. Are Oliver's
measurements correct? If not, write the correct measurements.

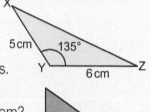

3 Here is a sketch of a right-angled triangle.
Does the right-angled triangle have a height of more than 4.5 cm?
Draw the triangle accurately to help you decide.

4 Draw triangle ABC with ∠ABC = 40°, AB = 7 cm, BC = 4 cm.

5 Draw a right-angled triangle with sides 6 cm, 8 cm and 10 cm.

6 Which of these descriptions cannot be triangles? Explain why.
Try to draw them to help you decide.

  A ∠XYZ = 110°, ∠YZX = 80°, YZ = 5 cm

  B ∠XYZ = 110°, XY = 8 cm, YZ = 3 cm

  C ∠XYZ = 110°, ∠YZX = 20°, XZ = 5 cm

  D ∠XYZ = 110°, XY = 8 cm, XZ = 3 cm

  E ∠XYZ = 110°, ∠YXZ = 40°, XY = 5 cm

Key points

- The angles on a straight line add up to 180°.
- The angles around a point add up to 360°.
- In a diagram, angles labelled with the same letter are the same size.

⚠ Purposeful practice 1

Work out the size of the missing angles in each sketch.

1

2

Reflect and reason

In **Q1** and **Q2** Jack says, '*a* is always 90° because the same letter means the angles are the same.' Use another example from Purposeful practice 1 to show why Jack's reasoning is incorrect.

⚠ Purposeful practice 2

Work out the size of the missing angles in each sketch.

1

2

3

Reflect and reason

In Purposeful practice 1 and Purposeful practice 2,
in which questions did you use only addition or subtraction to find the angles?
In which questions did you use only division?
Explain when you can use division to find missing angles.

1 Look at this sketch.

Dean says, 'Angle a is 50° because all of the angles are 50°.'
a Dean is incorrect. Explain why.
b Work out the correct size of angle a.

2 Look at this sketch.

Angle x in the sketch looks like a right angle.
Show that angle x cannot be a right angle.

3 In the sketches shown, which angle is bigger, a or b?
You must show your working.

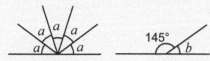

4 Work out the size of the obtuse angle and the reflex angle made by the hands of the clock.

5 Here are eight sectors from three whole circles.
Write which sectors make up each circle.

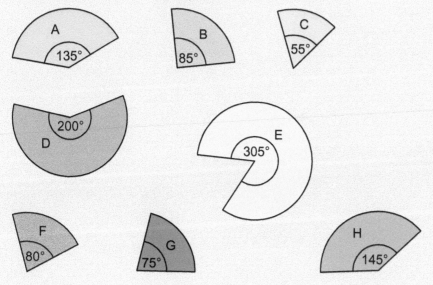

Key points

- The angles in a triangle add up to 180°.
- In an isosceles triangle, the angles at the base of the equal sides are equal.

△ Purposeful practice 1

1 Calculate the missing angles labelled *a* to *h* in these triangles.

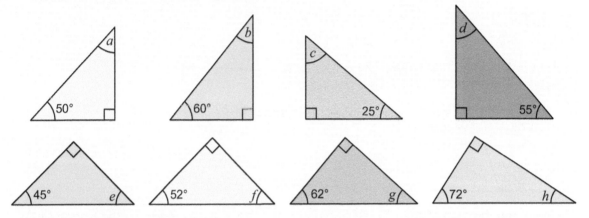

Reflect and reason

Is there a quick way to work out the missing angle in a right-angled triangle?

△ Purposeful practice 2

Calculate the missing angles in each triangle.

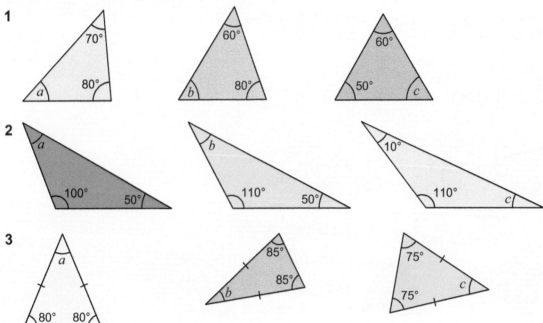

4

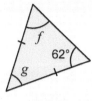

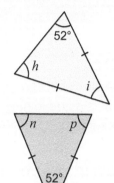

5

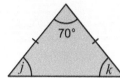

Reflect and reason

How many angles do you need to be given to find all the angles in a scalene triangle?
And what about an isosceles triangle?

⊠ Problem-solving practice

1 Two of the angles in a triangle are 42° and 75°.
Alex works out the missing angle in the triangle to be 73°.
Explain how you know Alex is wrong.

2 Work out the size of
the missing angles
in each sketch.

a

b

3 James and Steph work out the missing angles in the isosceles triangle.

James writes

$a = 70°$ because two angles are equal in an isosceles triangle.
$70 + 70 = 140$, so $b = 40°$

Steph writes

$a = b$ because two angles are equal in an isosceles triangle.
So $180 - 70 = 110$ and $110 \div 2 = 55$, so $a = b = 55°$

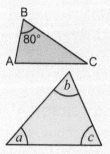

James and Steph are both incorrect.

a Explain what they have both done wrong.

b What are the sizes of angles a and b?

4 Can one of the angles in an equilateral triangle be 50°? Explain your answer.

5 Here is triangle ABC.
Angle BAC is three times greater than angle ACB.
Work out the size of angle BAC and angle ACB.

6 In this triangle, angle a is the smallest angle and c
is the largest angle.
Angle b is 10° greater than angle a and angle c
is 10° greater than angle b.
Work out the size of each angle.

Key points

- The properties of a shape are facts about its angles and sides.
- A diagonal is a line joining two opposite vertices.
- The angles in a quadrilateral add up to 360°.

△ Purposeful practice

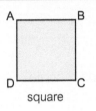
square

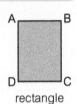
rectangle

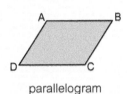
parallelogram

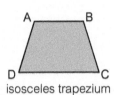
isosceles trapezium

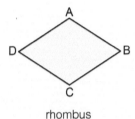
rhombus

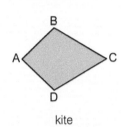
kite

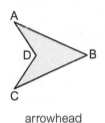
arrowhead

1 Which of the quadrilaterals have
  a no pairs of parallel sides
  b exactly one pair of parallel sides
  c two pairs of parallel sides?

2 Which of the quadrilaterals have
  a two pairs of equal sides, but not all four sides equal
  b all four sides equal
  c equal sides opposite each other
  d equal sides next to each other?

3 Which of the quadrilaterals have
  a four equal angles   **b** four right angles
  c exactly two pairs of equal angles   **d** exactly one pair of equal angles
  e their equal angles diagonally opposite each other?
  Use a protractor to measure and check your answers.

4 Write the side and angle properties of these quadrilaterals. Use your answers
to **Q1–3** to help you. The first one is started for you.
  a parallelogram   **b** rhombus
    two pairs of parallel sides...

Reflect and reason

Samira says a rhombus is a special type of parallelogram. Explain why she is correct.

Is a square a rhombus? Explain your answer.

Is a square a rectangle? Explain your answer.

1 Copy and complete the table using the words 'square', 'rectangle', 'parallelogram', 'rhombus', 'isosceles trapezium', 'kite' and 'arrowhead'.
Write the name of each quadrilateral in the box that best defines it. Boxes can contain more than one quadrilateral.

	Only one pair of equal angles	Two pairs of angles are equal	All four angles are equal
Sides next to each other are equal			
Only one pair of opposite sides are parallel		Isosceles trapezium	
Opposite sides are equal and parallel			
All four sides are equal			

2 Name each quadrilateral being described.
  a I have four equal sides and opposite equal angles, but not all my angles are equal.
  b All of my angles are right angles and when all my diagonals are drawn, they form right-angled triangles.
  c I have one pair of parallel sides and two pairs of equal angles.

3 Max has sketched these quadrilaterals.

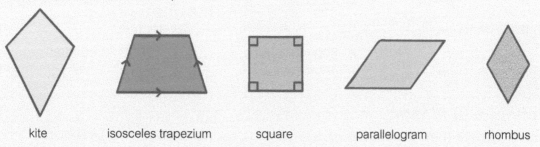

kite   isosceles trapezium   square   parallelogram   rhombus

He has forgotten to label his sketches with their measurements.
Match each quadrilateral to its measurements.
A 4 cm, 4 cm, 4 cm, 4 cm, 90°, 90°, 90°, 90°
B 4 cm, 6 cm, 4 cm, 6 cm, 80°, 100°, 80°, 100°
C 4 cm, 4 cm, 6 cm, 6 cm, 115°, 80°, 115°, 50°
D 4 cm, 4 cm, 4 cm, 4 cm, 80°, 100°, 80°, 100°
E 4 cm, 6 cm, 4 cm, 8 cm, 110°, 70°, 70°, 110°

4 Write the missing sides and angles for each sketch.

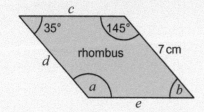

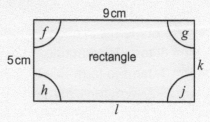

9 Sequences and graphs

Key points

- A number sequence is a set of numbers that follows a rule.
  Each number in a sequence is called a term.
- The term-to-term rule tells you how to get from one term to the next in a sequence.
- Sequences where the numbers increase are ascending sequences. Sequences where the numbers decrease are descending sequences.

△ Purposeful practice 1

1 Write the first four terms in each sequence.
   a First term 3, term-to-term rule '+ 2'   b First term 3, term-to-term rule '× 2'
   c First term 9, term-to-term rule '− 2'   d First term 24, term-to-term rule '÷ 2'
   e First term 20, term-to-term rule '+ 3'   f First term 20, term-to-term rule '− 3'
   g First term 1, term-to-term rule '× 3'   h First term 27, term-to-term rule '÷ 3'

2 Label each sequence in **Q1** 'ascending' or 'descending'.

3 Write the term-to-term rule and the next two terms in each sequence.
   a 5, 8, 11, ...   b 12, 9, 6, ...   c 3, 8, 13, ...
   d 27, 22, 17, ...   e 1000, 998, 996, ...   f 526, 528, 530, ...
   g 2000, 1000, 500, ...   h 1, 2, 4, ...   i $\frac{1}{2}$, 1, 2, ...
   j 10, 20, 40, ...   k 800, 400, 200, ...   l 10 000, 9990 9980, ...
   m 10 000, 1000, 100, ... n 2, 20, 200, ...   o 2000, 2010, 2020, ...

Reflect and reason

Which types of term-to-term rule give ascending sequences? Which types give descending sequences?

How can you use this to help you find the term-to-term rules in **Q3**?

△ Purposeful practice 2

1 Write the first four terms in each sequence.
   a First term 6, term-to-term rule '− 1'   b First term 6, term-to-term rule '− 2'
   c First term 6, term-to-term rule '− 3'   d First term 6, term-to-term rule '− 6'
   e First term −5, term-to-term rule '+ 5'   f First term −5, term-to-term rule '+ 4'
   g First term −5, term-to-term rule '+ 2'   h First term −5, term-to-term rule '+ 1'

2 Write the first four terms in each sequence.
   a First term 3, term-to-term rule '− 2'   b First term 2, term-to-term rule '− 2'
   c First term 1, term-to-term rule '− 2'   d First term −1, term-to-term rule '− 2'
   e First term −2, term-to-term rule '− 2'   f First term −2, term-to-term rule '− 3'
   g First term −2, term-to-term rule '− 5'

3 Write the first four terms in each sequence.

    a First term 7, term-to-term rule '+ $\frac{1}{2}$'   **b** First term 7, term-to-term rule '+ 0.2'

    c First term 7, term-to-term rule '− 0.3'   **d** First term 7, term-to-term rule '−$\frac{1}{2}$'

    e First term 20, term-to-term rule '+ 0.1'   **f** First term 20, term-to-term rule '× 0.1'

    g First term 8.4, term-to-term rule '− 2'   **h** First term 8.4, term-to-term rule '÷ 2'

Reflect and reason

Look at your answer to **Q3f**. When does a term-to-term rule where you multiply by a number give a descending sequence?

Does this change your answers to the Reflect and reason questions in Purposeful practice 1?

⊠ Problem-solving practice

1 Amil is given the sequence 1, 5, 25, 125, ...
Amil says, 'The term-to-term rule for the sequence is + 4.'
Is Amil correct? Explain your answer.

2 Work out the missing terms in each sequence.

    a 8, 11, ☐, 17, ☐, ...   **b** 100, ☐, 80, ☐, 60, ...   **c** 12, 17, ☐, ☐, 32, ...

    d −2, 5, ☐, 19, ☐, ...   **e** −5, ☐, −9, ☐, −13, ...   **f** 9.2, ☐, ☐, 7.4, 6.8, ...

3 The first four terms of a sequence are 7, 11, 15, 19
Ceri says, '36 will be in the sequence.' Is Ceri correct? Explain your answer.

4 Mrs Brown gives her students the sequence 23, 18, 13, 8, 3, ...
She asks her students to write the next two terms of the sequence.

Student A writes	Student B writes	Student C writes
−8, −13	−3, −8	−2, −7

Which student is correct? Explain your answer.

5 The term-to-term rule of a sequence is '− 8'.
The first term of the sequence is 50.
How many positive terms does the sequence have?

6 Alesha uses five of these numbers to make an ascending sequence.
What could Alesha's sequence be?
4.2   4.4   4.5   4.7   4.8   4.9   5.0   5.1   5.3   5.4

7 A sequence begins 1, 10, ...

    a What could the next term be? Give two possible answers.

    b What is the term-to-term rule for each of your sequences?

    c Write the next three terms for each of your sequences.

8 Write a first term and a term-to-term rule for a descending sequence that includes the term 8.3

9 The numbers in two sequences have become mixed up. These are the numbers.
40   34   42   26   46   38   50   33   54   47

One sequence is an ascending sequence, the other is descending.
One sequence has a term-to-term rule of '+ 7'.
The other sequence has a first term of 50.
Write both sequences.

Key point

- You can draw the next pattern in a sequence by working out how the pattern grows.

△ Purposeful practice 1

For each pattern sequence

a find the first number term

c find the term-to-term rule

b find the first three number terms

d describe how the sequence grows

The first one is done for you.

1

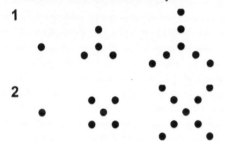

a First term is 1 **b** 1, 4, 7 **c** + 3

d There is 1 dot in the first pattern. 3 dots are added each time.

2

3

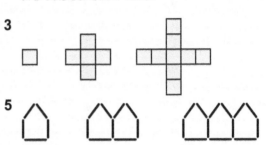

4 △ ▷▽ ▷▽△

5 ⌂ ⌂⌂ ⌂⌂⌂

Reflect and reason

How can you describe how a pattern grows?

△ Purposeful practice 2

For each sequence of growing rectangles, write the multiplication for the

a 3rd rectangle **b** 4th rectangle **c** 10th rectangle

1 2 × 1   2 × 2   2 × _   _ × _

2 3 × 1   3 × 2   3 × _   _ × _

3 2 × 1   3 × 2   4 × _   _ × _

4 2 × 1   4 × 2   6 × _   _ × _

Reflect and reason

In **Q3**, describe the sequence of the first numbers in the multiplications, and the sequence in the second numbers.

How can you use sequences to find the multiplications in **Q4**?

⊠ Problem-solving practice

1 The first three patterns of some sequences are shown.
Write the number of dots in the fifth pattern for each sequence. Choose your answer
from these numbers: 11 15 16 17

A ••• ••• ••• ••• •••   B •   •• ••   ••• •••

C •   •   •   D •   •   •

2 Work out the number of lines in the 10th
pattern of this sequence.

3 Can Shahid use exactly 14 rods to make a pattern
in this sequence?
Explain your answer.

4 Will there be a 9 × 10 rectangle in this sequence of growing rectangles?
Explain your answer.

4 × 1   4 × ☐   ☐ × ☐   ☐ × ☐

5 Each pattern in this sequence is made using counters.

a How many patterns in the sequence can be made in total using 50 counters?
b How many counters will be left over?

6 Pattern 4 and Pattern 5 of four different sequences are shown.
Which of the sequences have three squares in their first pattern?

A Pattern 4   Pattern 5   B Pattern 4   Pattern 5

C Pattern 4   Pattern 5   D Pattern 4   Pattern 5

7 Each pattern in this sequence is made using square
tiles. How many patterns in the sequence use
between 25 and 50 squares each?

Key point

- The midpoint of a line segment is the point exactly in the middle.

△ Purposeful practice 1

For each function machine

a copy and complete the table of values

x	0	1	2	3	4	5
y						

b describe the sequence of the y-values
(Give the first term and the term-to-term rule.)

c draw a coordinate grid with x and y-axes from –8 to 8 and plot the points

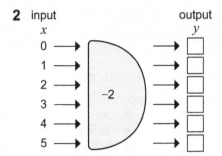

1 input   output

2 input   output

Reflect and reason

What is the same about the sequences of y-values in **Q1** and **Q2**? What is different?

What is the same about the graphs in **Q1** and **Q2**? What is different? How is the difference in the two sequences shown in the two graphs?

△ Purposeful practice 2

1 Find the midpoint of each line segment shown in the graph. Copy and complete the table to record your results.

Line segment	Beginning point	Endpoint	Midpoint
AB	(2, 8)	(2, 2)	
CD			

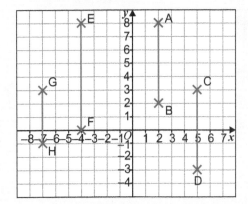

2 Find the midpoint of each line segment.
Copy and complete the table to record your
results.

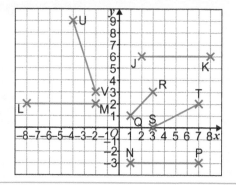

Line segment	Beginning point	Endpoint	Midpoint
JK	(2, 6)		
LM			

Reflect and reason

How can you find the coordinates of the midpoint first by looking at the coordinates of
the beginning and endpoints?

⊠ Problem-solving practice

1 Paul is asked to copy and complete
a function machine and plot the
points on a coordinate grid.

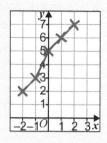

a How do you know from looking
at the graph that Paul has made
a mistake?

b Which *y*-coordinates are wrong?
What should the values be?

c Plot the correct points on a copy of the coordinate grid.

d When the line is extended, does the point (5, 10) lie on the line? Explain why.

2 M is the midpoint of PQ.
The diagram shows points P and M.
What are the coordinates of Q?

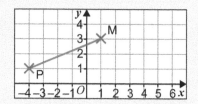

3 Work out the midpoint of each line segment. You must show your working.

a

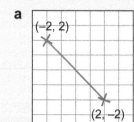

b

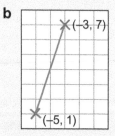

c

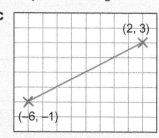

4 Work out the midpoint of each line segment AB with the given coordinates.
You must show your working.

   a A(0, 0) and B(6, 6)   **b** A(0, 4) and B(4, 0)

   c A(2, 2) and B(6, 6)   **d** A(5, 3) and B(1, 7)

Key points

- An arithmetic sequence goes up or down in equal steps.
- You can describe an arithmetic sequence using the first term and the common difference (the difference between terms).

▲ Purposeful practice 1

1 Find the term-to-term rule for each sequence.
Write whether or not the sequence is arithmetic.

   a 2, 5, 8, 11, ...
   b 2, 6, 10, 14, ...
   c 2, 0, −2, −4, ...
   d −4, −1, 2, 5, ...
   e −4, −2, 0, 2, ...
   f 1, 2, 3, 4, ...
   g 1, 2, 4, 8, ...
   h 1, 3, 9, 27, ...
   i 1, 3, 5, 7, ...
   j 100, 10, 1, 0.1, ...
   k 60, 30, 15, 7.5, ...
   l 60, 30, 0, −30, ...

2 Write the first four terms of each sequence.
Write whether or not the sequence is arithmetic.

   a First term 3, term-to-term rule multiply by 2
   b First term 3, term-to-term rule multiply by 2 and add 1
   c First term 3, term-to-term rule multiply by 2 and subtract 1
   d First term 3, term-to-term rule add 1 and multiply by 2
   e First term 3, term-to-term rule subtract 1 and multiply by 2

> ## Reflect and reason
> How can you tell from its term-to-term rule if a sequence is arithmetic?

▲ Purposeful practice 2

For each pattern sequence

a copy and complete the table

b work out the number of items (dots, sticks or squares) in the 10th pattern

The first one has been started for you.

Pattern number	1	2	3	4
Sequence				

1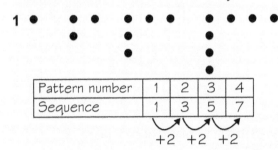

Pattern number	1	2	3	4
Sequence	1	3	5	7

+2 +2 +2

1st pattern   1
2nd pattern $1 + 1 \times 2 = 3$
3rd pattern $1 + 2 \times 2 = 5$
4th pattern $1 + 3 \times 2 = \square$
10th pattern $1 + 9 \times \square = \square$

2

3 ∧ ∧∕ ∧∕∖ ∧∕∖∕

4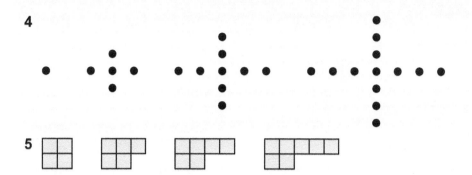

5

Reflect and reason

For **Q1–5**, Hayley says, 'The 10th term is always first term + 9 × common difference.'
Use examples from **Q1–5** to show she is correct.

⊠ Problem-solving practice

1 Harry is given the sequence 1, 3, 7, 15, ...
Harry says, 'The sequence is not an arithmetic sequence.'
Is he correct? Explain your answer.

2 The first term of an arithmetic sequence is 3.
The common difference of the sequence is + 10.
Is 65 in the sequence? Explain your answer.

3 The first term of the sequence is −15.
The term-to-term rule of a sequence is '+ 2'.
How many negative terms does the sequence have?

4 Work out the missing terms in each arithmetic sequence.
   a 2, 9, ☐, ☐, ☐, ...   **b** 100, ☐, ☐, ☐, 76, ...
   c ☐, ☐, ☐, 1, −4, ...   **d** 5.0, ☐, ☐, ☐, 3.8, ...

5 The first three patterns of some sequences are shown. Choose, from these numbers, the number of squares in the tenth pattern for each sequence: | 37   31   30   21 |

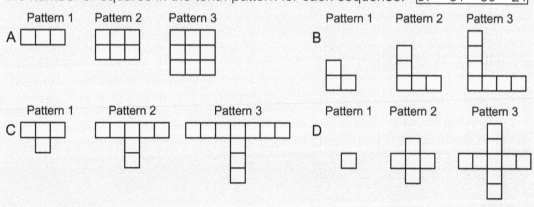

6 Each pattern in this sequence is made using hexagons.
Work out the number of hexagons in the 10th pattern.

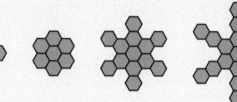

Key points

- The equation $y = 2$ means the y-coordinate is always 2, whatever the x-coordinate is. The line is parallel to the x-axis.
- The equation $x = 3$ means the x-coordinate is always 3, whatever the y-coordinate is. This line is parallel to the y-axis.

Purposeful practice 1

1 Write the equation of the lines labelled A to H.

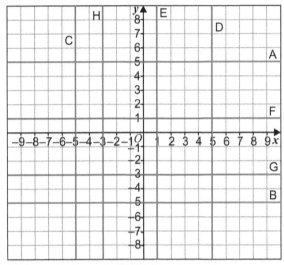

2 Write another name for the line
   a $y = 0$ **b** $x = 0$

Reflect and reason

Jim says, 'The equation of line H in **Q1** is $y = -3$, because it is parallel to the y-axis.' Explain why Jim is incorrect.

Purposeful practice 2

1 Copy and complete each table of values for
   a $y = x$

x	−5	−4	−3	−2	−1	0	1	2	3	4	5
y											

   b $y = -x$

x	−5	−4	−3	−2	−1	0	1	2	3	4	5
y	5					0					−5

   c Draw the graphs of $y = x$ and $y = -x$ on a copy of the axes in Purposeful practice 1 **Q1**.

2 Copy and complete this table of values for each equation.

a $y = x + 1$
b $y = 2x$
c $y = 2x + 1$

x	0	1	2	3	4
y					

Draw a graph for each equation on the same coordinate grid. Draw the coordinate grid with x-axis from –1 to 5 and y-axis from –2 to 10.

Reflect and reason

In **Q1**, what is the same and what is different about the graphs of $y = x$ and $y = -x$?

In **Q2**, what is the same and what is different about the graphs of $y = 2x$ and $y = 2x + 1$?

⊠ Problem-solving practice

1 Match each line with its equation.

a $x = 2$ **b** $y = 2$ **c** $x = 0$
d $y = 0$ **e** $x = 4$ **f** $y = 4$
g $x = -2$ **h** $y = -2$

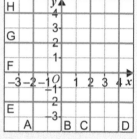

2 Which of these coordinates lie on the line $x = 5$? Explain your answer.

(0, 1)   (5, 3)   (−5, 5)   (−5, −5)   (5, 5)   (5, 0)   (0, 5)   (5, −5)

3 Sonia is asked to draw and label the graphs of $y = x$ and $y = -x$.

Here is Sonia's graph:
Is Sonia correct? Explain why or why not.

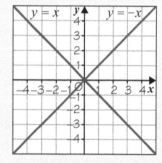

4 a Copy and complete this table of values for the graph.

x	0	1	2	3	4	5
y						

b Copy and complete the sentence.
The y-values go up by ___ each time.

c Will the point (8, 24) lie on the line? Explain why or why not.

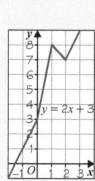

5 This is Jack's graph of $y = 2x + 3$.

a Which coordinate do you think is most likely to be wrong? Explain why.

b Draw the correct graph of $y = 2x + 3$.

Key points

- Each term in a sequence has a position. The first term is in position 1, the second term is in position 2, the third term is in position 3 and so on.
- The position-to-term rule helps you work out a term when you know its position.
- You use algebra to write the position-to-term rule. It is called the nth term because it tells you how to work out the term at position n (any position).

Purposeful practice 1

Work out the first five terms of each sequence from the position-to-term rule.

1 $2n$ **2** $4n$ **3** $7n$ **4** $10n$

Reflect and reason

What is the nth term for the multiples of 2? What is the nth term for the multiples of 9? What sequence has nth term $5n$?

Purposeful practice 2

For each position-to-term rule

i work out the first five terms in the sequence

ii write the common difference of the sequence

1 a $4n$ **b** $4n + 1$ **c** $4n - 1$ **d** $4n + 3$
2 a $3n$ **b** $3n + 2$ **c** $3n - 2$ **d** $3n - 1$
3 a $6n$ **b** $6n + 1$ **c** $6n + 5$ **d** $6n - 1$

Reflect and reason

What is the relationship between the common difference of a sequence and the number before the n in its nth term?

Purposeful practice 3

For each position-to-term rule

i work out the first five terms in the sequence

ii describe the sequence as 'multiples of ___, plus/subtract___'

1 a $2n$ **b** $2n + 1$ **c** $2n + 3$ **d** $2n - 3$ **e** $2n - 1$
2 a $5n$ **b** $5n + 1$ **c** $5n + 2$ **d** $5n - 2$ **e** $5n - 1$

Reflect and reason

What do you notice about the numbers in the sequences in **Q2**?

Which of these sequences are related to multiples of 5? Explain your answer.

A 5, 12, 19, 26, 33, ...   B 8, 13, 18, 23, 28, ...
C 12, 17, 22, 27, 32, ...   D 5, 9, 15, 19, 25, ...

1 Matt is asked to write the first five terms of the sequence with nth term $3n$.
Matt writes

3, 6, 9, 13, 16

Is Matt correct? Explain why.

2 Which of these sequences has nth term $11n$?
A 11, 21, 31, 41, 51, ...
B 11, 12, 13, 14, 15, ...
C 11, 111, 1111, 11 111, ...
D 11, 22, 33, 44, 55, ...

3 The nth term of a sequence is $6n$.
How many terms are between 40 and 70?

4 Match each sequence A–F to its nth term G–L.
A 7, 11, 15, 19, ...   G $3n$
B 3, 6, 9, 12, ...   H $3n + 4$
C 1, 5, 9, 13, ...   I $3n - 1$
D 7, 10, 13, 16, ...   J $4n$
E 4, 8, 12, 16, ...   K $4n + 3$
F 2, 5, 8, 11, ...   L $4n - 3$

5 The nth term of a sequence is $5n - 3$.
What is the 10th term of the sequence?

6 Damien says, 'The sequence with nth term $7n + 3$ only has even numbers in the sequence.'
Give an example to show Damien is wrong.

7 The nth term of a sequence is $2n + 3$.
Is 30 in the sequence? Explain your answer.

8 The nth term of a sequence is $2n - 9$.
How many negative terms are there in the sequence?

9 What is the nth term of a sequence where the terms are
a multiples of 7
b 2 less than each multiple of 5
c 6 more than each multiple of 5?

10 Which of these sequences has nth term $3n + 2$?
A 3, 5, 7, 9, 11, ...
B 5, 7, 9, 11, 13, ...
C 3, 6, 9, 12, 15, ...
D 5, 8, 11, 14, 17, ...

11 Which of these describes a sequence which has nth term $2n + 3$? Explain why.
A The first term is 5 and the common difference is + 2
B The first term is 2 and the common difference is + 2
C The first term is 3 and the common difference is + 2
D The first term is 6 and the common difference is + 2

10 Transformations

Key points

- Shapes are congruent if they are the same shape and size.
- In congruent shapes, corresponding sides (matching sides) and corresponding angles (matching angles) are equal.
- An enlargement transforms a shape. In maths, it is a type of transformation. When enlarging a shape, you multiply all its side lengths by the same number. The number you multiply by is called the scale factor.

△ Purposeful practice 1

1 Which shapes are congruent to shape A?

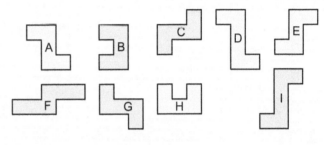

2 Which triangles are congruent?

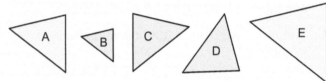

Reflect and reason

Which of these statements about congruent shapes are true? They

A have the same angles   B are the same colour   C are the same size

△ Purposeful practice 2

Shapes 1 and 2 are congruent. Shapes 3 and 4 are congruent.

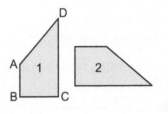
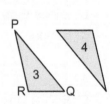

1 Trace shape 2 and label the vertices E, F, G and H so that AB and EF are corresponding sides, BC and FG are corresponding sides, and CD and GH are corresponding sides.

2 What is the corresponding side to AD?

3 Trace shape 4 and label the vertices S, T and U so that PQ and ST are corresponding sides and angle R and angle U are corresponding angles.

Reflect and reason

How did tracing shapes 2 and 4 help you find corresponding sides and angles?

Write the scale factor of enlargement from A to B for each pair of shapes.

1 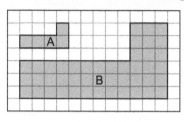   **2** 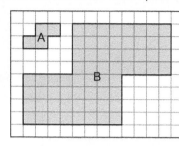   **3**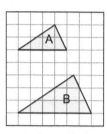

Reflect and reason

Henry says, 'This shape is an enlargement of shape A in **Q1** by scale factor 2.'

Is he correct? Explain your answer.

⊠ **Problem-solving practice**

1 Are these pairs of shapes congruent? Explain why or why not.

a 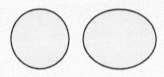   **b**

2 A triangle has perimeter 18 cm. The triangle is enlarged by scale factor 5. What is the perimeter of the enlarged triangle?

3 Which of these triangles are enlargements of triangle A? Explain why.

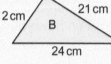   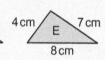

4 Ewan enlarges shape A by scale factor 2. Is Ewan correct? Give reasons for your answer.

5 Explain why shape B is an enlargement of shape A.

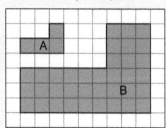

Key points

• A shape has line symmetry if one half folds exactly on top of the other half.
  The dashed line is called a line of symmetry or mirror line.

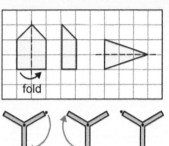

fold

• A shape has rotational symmetry if it looks the same more than once in a full turn.
  This shape looks the same in three positions, so it has rotational symmetry of order 3.

• A shape that does not look the same when turned has no rotational symmetry.

△ Purposeful practice 1

1 Copy these shapes. Draw the lines of symmetry on each shape.

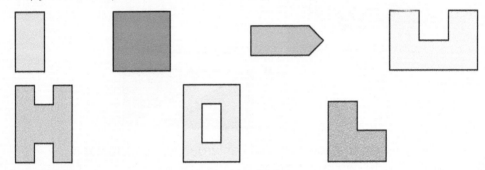

Reflect and reason

Leo draws lines of symmetry on this rectangle and parallelogram.

Are his lines of symmetry on these shapes correct? Explain how you know.

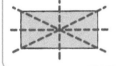

△ Purposeful practice 2

For each triangle, write

a the number of lines of symmetry

b the order of rotational symmetry

1

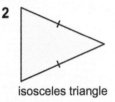

scalene triangle

2

isosceles triangle

3

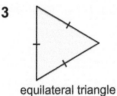

equilateral triangle

4

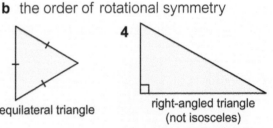

right-angled triangle
(not isosceles)

Reflect and reason

Is it possible to draw a right-angled triangle with one line of symmetry?
Is it possible to draw a right-angled triangle with rotational symmetry of order 3?
Draw examples to explain your answers.

These are all isosceles triangles. Find the missing sides and angles.

1

2

3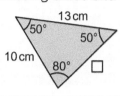

4

Reflect and reason

How can lines of symmetry help when finding missing sides and angles in an isosceles triangle?

⊠ Problem-solving practice

1 Say whether each statement is true or false.
Explain your answers.

  a A scalene triangle has no lines of symmetry.

  b An isosceles triangle has three lines of symmetry.

  c An equilateral triangle has three lines of symmetry.

  d A rhombus has two lines of symmetry.

  e A rectangle has four lines of symmetry.

2 Finn draws all the lines of symmetry on a rhombus and a kite.

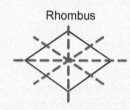 Rhombus

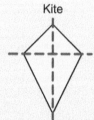 Kite

  a Are his lines correct? Explain your answer.

Finn then says, 'A rhombus has rotational symmetry order 4 and a kite has rotational symmetry order 2.'

  b Is he correct? Explain your answer.

3 Copy and shade two squares on each diagram so that the order of rotational symmetry is correct.

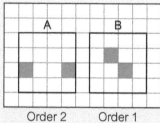

Order 2   Order 1

4 This hexagon is made up of equilateral triangles.
On separate copies of the hexagon, shade triangles so that it has

  a no lines of symmetry

  b only two lines of symmetry

  c rotational symmetry of order 2

  d rotational symmetry of order 3

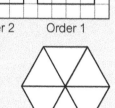

5 Draw a shape with one line of symmetry and no rotational symmetry.

Key points

- A reflection is a type of transformation. You reflect shapes in a mirror line. All points on the object are the same distance from the mirror line as the corresponding points on the image, but on the opposite side.
- Lines of reflection on coordinate grids can be described by their equations.
- To reflect a shape in the line $y = x$ or $y = -x$, count the distance from each vertex of the shape to the line, then count the same again on the other side of the line.

⚠ Purposeful practice 1

Copy each pair of shapes. Draw in the mirror line for each pair.

1 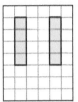 2 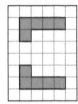 3 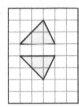 4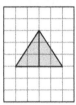

Reflect and reason

Why is the dotted line that shows where a shape is reflected called the mirror line?

⚠ Purposeful practice 2

1 Which point is a reflection of
   a A in the x-axis
   b B in the y-axis
   c C in the x-axis
   d D in line $x = 2$
   e E in line $y = -1$
   f F in line $x = \frac{1}{2}$?

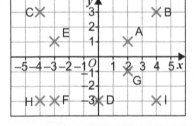

2 Copy the grid and shape A.
   Draw a reflection of shape A in the
   a x-axis. Label the image B.
   b y-axis. Label the image C.
   c line $y = -x$. Label the image D.
   d line $y = x$. Label the image E.
   e line $x = -1$. Label the image F.

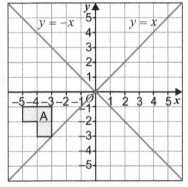

Reflect and reason

After answering **Q2**, Antony writes

F is a reflection of C in the line $x = 3$ and E is a reflection of F in the line $x = 1$

Is Antony correct? Explain your answers for each statement.

1 Which is the correct reflection? Explain why.

A   B   C

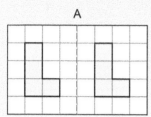 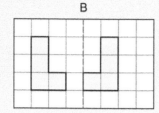 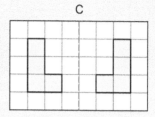

2 Maylia is asked to reflect the triangle A in the line $y = x$.
   Has Maylia drawn a correct reflection?
   Explain your answer.

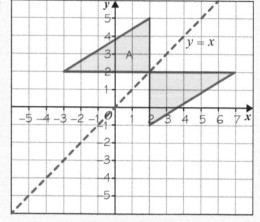

3 The diagram shows six triangles.
   Copy and complete each sentence.
   a B is a reflection of A in the line _____.
   b E is a reflection of D in the line _____.
   c C is a reflection of F in the line _____.
   d B is a reflection of C in the line _____.
   e D is a reflection of A in the line _____.

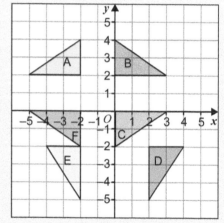

4 Copy the diagram.
   a Reflect shape A in the line $y = -x$. Label it B.
     Draw the cross shown on shape A on the
     corresponding corner of shape B.
   b Write the coordinates of the point marked with
     a cross in shape A.
   c Write the coordinates of the point marked with
     a cross in shape B.
   d What is the connection between the
     coordinates in parts b and c?
   e Does this connection work for all
     corresponding coordinates on the shapes?
     Give examples to explain your answer.

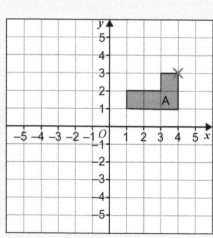

Key points

- A rotation is a type of transformation. You rotate a shape by turning it around a point, called the centre of rotation. To describe a rotation, you also need to give the angle and direction (clockwise or anticlockwise).
- A rotation of 180° is the same in a clockwise and anticlockwise direction. Therefore, there is no need to state the direction for a rotation of 180°.

△ Purposeful practice 1

1 Each grey shape has been rotated about the centre of rotation marked with a cross. Match each rotation to one of these descriptions of rotation.

| 90° clockwise | 90° anticlockwise | 180° |

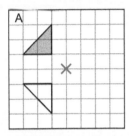
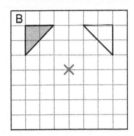

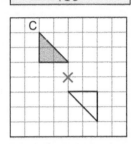

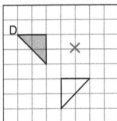
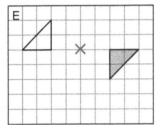
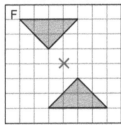

2 Copy the grid and the triangle.

  a On your copy, rotate the triangle

    i 90° anticlockwise about (3, 3). Label the image A.

    ii 90° anticlockwise about (2, 2). Label the image B.

    iii 90° anticlockwise about (1, 1). Label the image C.

    iv 180° about (3, 3). Label the image D.

    v 180° about (2, 2). Label the image E.

    vi 180° about (1, 1). Label the image F.

  b Write the coordinates of the corners of each triangle A, B, C, D, E, F.

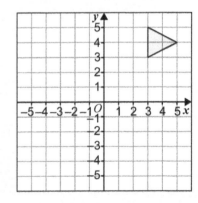

Reflect and reason

Predict the coordinates of the triangle in **Q2** rotated

  90° anticlockwise about (0, 0)

  180° about (0, 0)

Check your prediction by carrying out the rotations.

Look at the shapes on the grid.
Describe these rotations.

1 A onto B   **2** A onto C

3 B onto D   **4** B onto E

5 D onto F

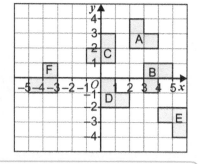

Reflect and reason

Danny says, 'A rotation of any shape 180° about (0, 0) is the same as reflecting the shape in the x-axis.'

Is Danny correct? Draw a grid, a shape and a rotation to explain your answer.

⊠ Problem-solving practice

1 Joe is asked to rotate each shaded shape 90° anticlockwise around the point marked with a cross. His answers are shown.

   a Joe is incorrect. Explain why.

   b Copy the shaded shapes and show what Joe should have drawn.

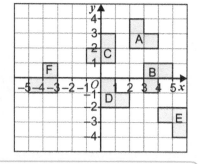

2 Ashleigh is asked to describe the rotation of shape A onto B.

Ashleigh says, 'Shape B is a rotation of shape A 180° about (1, 2).'

Is Ashleigh correct? Explain your answer.

You may use a diagram or coordinates in your explanation.

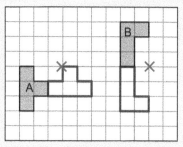

3 a Match each description to the correct pair of shapes (one pair won't be used).

    i 180° rotation about (0, 0)

    ii 90° rotation clockwise about (2, 2)

    iii 180° rotation about (0, 1)

    iv 90° rotation anticlockwise about (−1, −4)

    v 90° rotation clockwise about (0, 0)

    vi 180° rotation about (0, −1)

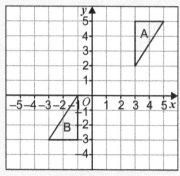

| C onto G | G onto D | F onto G | B onto D |

| A onto E | E onto F | B onto C |

   b Describe the rotation for the pair of shapes you have left.

Key points

- A translation is a type of transformation. A translation of a 2D shape is a slide across a flat surface. To describe a translation you need to give the movement left or right, followed by the movement up or down.
- Reflections, rotations and translations are all types of transformation.

Purposeful practice 1

1 Describe each translation from X to

   a A   **b** B   **c** C   **d** D

   e E   **f** F   **g** G   **h** H

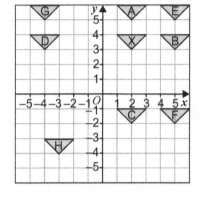

2 Copy the grid and the trapezium. Extend the axes so they go from −7 to 7 in both directions.

   Translate trapezium A

   a 4 squares right. Label the image B.

   b 4 squares right and 2 squares up. Label the image C.

   c 8 squares right and 2 squares up. Label the image D.

   d 8 squares right and 6 squares down. Label the image E.

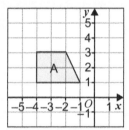

Reflect and reason

Faisal says, 'I have translated triangle 1 to triangle 2 by moving it 2 squares right and 1 square down.'
What two mistakes has he made?

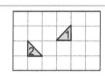

Purposeful practice 2

Match each description in **Q1–Q6** to the correct two-step transformation A–F.

   A Transformation from P to Q   B Transformation from Q to S

   C Transformation from R to S   D Transformation from P to T

   E Transformation from Q to R   F Transformation from T to S

1 Reflection in $x = 2$ followed by a translation 5 down

2 Translation 2 squares left followed by a reflection in $y = 4$

3 Rotation 90° anticlockwise about (8, 6) followed by a translation 2 squares down

4 Reflection in $y = 2$ followed by a rotation 90° anticlockwise about (6, 4)

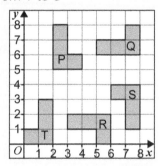

5 Rotation 180° about (2, 2) followed by a reflection in $x = 5$

6 Rotation 90° anticlockwise about (4, 8) followed by a translation 1 square right.

Reflect and reason

Alice says, 'To answer the questions in this exercise, I began by looking for shapes that were reflections, ignoring their position. This helped me to identify the transformations described by **Q1** and **Q2**, but not **Q4** and **Q5**.'

Why was this the case?

Explain your strategy for answering this question.

⊠ Problem-solving practice

1 Priya is asked to translate rectangle A 3 squares right and 2 squares up. Her answer is shown.

Priya says, 'This is the translation of rectangle A, because there are 3 squares between the rectangles horizontally, and 2 squares vertically.'

Priya is incorrect. Explain why.

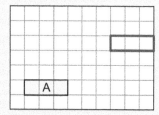

2 Are triangles Q and R translations of triangle P? Explain your answer in each case.

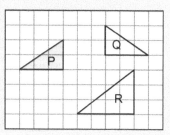

3 **a** Describe the translation that moves shape A to B.

b Describe the translation that moves shape B to A.

c What do you notice about your answers to parts **a** and **b**? Does this work for other translations? Draw two different examples.

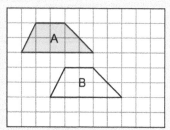

4 Look at the diagram.
Write the two shapes that each translation is describing. The first one is done for you.

a 4 squares left   *C onto B*

b 5 squares right

c 6 squares up

d 2 squares right and 1 square up

e 1 square left and 1 square down

f 5 squares left and 3 squares down

g 3 squares right and 1 square down

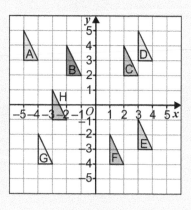

Mixed exercises C

Mixed problem-solving practice C

1 **a** Write the coordinates of point A.
 b Write the coordinates of point B.
 c Write the coordinates of the midpoint of BC.
 d What type of angle is angle BAC?
 A, B and C are three vertices of a parallelogram.
 e i How many possible parallelograms could there be
 with these three vertices?
   ii Write the coordinates of the fourth vertex in each of
   these parallelograms.

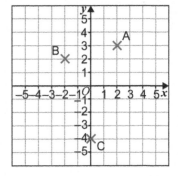

2 Here is a list of five types of quadrilateral.
  trapezium   parallelogram   square   rhombus   rectangle
  Write the name of the quadrilateral from this list for which all the following apply.
   The corners are not right angles.
   The quadrilateral has rotational symmetry of order 2.
   The quadrilateral has no lines of symmetry.

3 Draw a coordinate grid with x- and y-axes from -7 to $+7$.
  a Plot the points A(–3, 5), B(–1, 4), C(–3, 1) and D(–5, 4) and join them to make
  quadrilateral ABCD.
  b What type of quadrilateral is ABCD?
  c Reflect ABCD in the line $y = -1$.

4 Describe fully the transformation that maps shape A onto shape B in each diagram.
  a
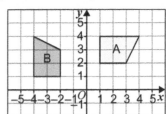
  b

5 Work out the size of the angle marked x in each diagram.
  You must show your working.
  a
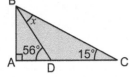
  b
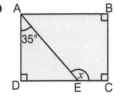
  c
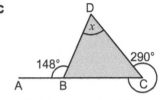

  ABC is a right-angled triangle.   ABCD is a rectangle.   ABC is a straight line.
  ADC is a straight line.   E is a point on DC.

6 This shape is made from an equilateral triangle and three congruent isosceles triangles.

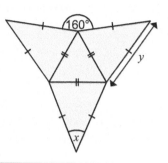

   a Work out the size of the angle marked x in the diagram. Give reasons for your answer.

   b You are told that the perimeter of the shape is 84 cm. Explain how you can use this information to work out the length y.

7 The diagram shows triangle A drawn on a grid.

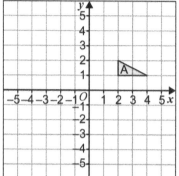

Sunnil reflects triangle A in the y-axis to get triangle B. He then reflects triangle B in the line $y = x$ to get triangle C.

Maria reflects triangle A in the line $y = x$ to get triangle D.

She then reflects triangle D in the y-axis to get triangle E.

Maria says, 'Triangle E is in the same position as triangle C.'

Is she correct? You must show how you get your answer.

8 Here are some patterns in a sequence, made from lines and circles.

1   2   3   4   5   6

7   8   20

   a Draw pattern number 9.
   b Draw pattern number 15. Use pattern number 20 to help you.
   c Copy and complete the table.

Pattern number	1	2	3	4	5	6	7	8	9	10
Number of lines	4	7	10							

Hamish wants to work out how many lines make pattern 30.

   d Write a method he can use.
   e How many lines are in pattern number 30?
   f How many circles are in pattern number 30?

Hamish uses this pattern for a wallpaper design.
Hamish wants a single spiral pattern to fit in one width of the wallpaper.
Each square made by lines and a circle has a side length of 6.5 cm.
The wallpaper roll is 0.53 m wide.

   g How many whole squares will fit across the width of the wallpaper?
   h How many lines are there in the maximum-size spiral that will fit across the width of the wallpaper?

Answers

1 Analysing and displaying data

1.1 Mode, median and range

Purposeful practice 1

1 a 4	**b** 4	**c** 4	**d** 3	**e** 4	**f** 4
2 a 5	**b** 5	**c** 6	**d** 6	**e** 10	**f** 9
3 a 14.5	**b** 15	**c** 15.5	**d** 24	**e** 24.5	**f** 25
g 25	**h** 25.5				

Purposeful practice 2

1 17	**2** 22	**3** 21	**4** 20
5 19	**6** 18	**7** 21	**8** 21
9 21	**10** 18	**11** 21	**12** 27

Purposeful practice 3

1 a 0	**b** 1	**c** 2	**d** 3	**e** 2	**f** 2
g 2	**h** 7	**i** 2			
2 a 9	**b** 9	**c** 9	**d** 11	**e** 12	**f** 15
g 15	**h** 15				

Problem-solving practice

1 a 7   **b** 7   **c** 7
2 a 4   **b** 4   **c** 5
3 Taylor did not order the numbers first. When the numbers are in order the correct median is 14.
4 a 5   **b** 7
  c No this doesn't change the range as the largest and smallest shoe sizes have not changed.
  d 2 or 11
5 3 or 11   **6** 2, 7, 9, 9

1.2 Displaying data

Purposeful practice 1

1

Colour	Tally	Frequency
ginger	JHT	5
black	JHT JHT JHT	15
tabby	JHT JHT	10
white	III	3

2   Colours of cats

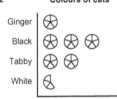

Key: ⊗ represents 5 cats

3

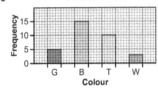

4

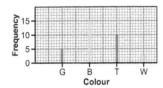

Purposeful practice 2

1 Mode 7 red sweets, range 4
2 Mode strawberry, no range.

Problem-solving practice

1 a

Sport	Frequency
football	12
netball	9
swimming	**5**
tennis	**4**

  b The bar chart should have a bar with a height of 12 added for football, and a bar with a height of 9 added for netball.
2 a 16   **b** 14
  c The pictogram should have $\frac{1}{4}$ of a full square drawn for Thursday and 3 full squares drawn for Friday.
  d Friday
3 a 1p   **b** 20p   **c** 4   **d** 90

1.3 Grouping data

Purposeful practice 1

1 30, 20 and 40 are in two groups
2 Students' own answers based on their categories used in the first column. For example,

Number of likes	Tally	Frequency
0–10	I	1
11–20	III	3
21–30	I	1
31–40	III	3
41–50	I	1

Purposeful practice 2

1

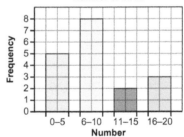

2

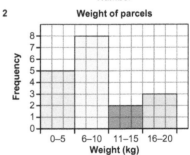

Problem-solving practice

1 Table A because it is in groups of 10. The groups in table B overlap and the last group in table C is not a group of 10.

2

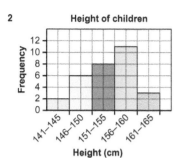

Height of children

3 a

Age (in years)	Frequency
21–30	7
31–40	13
41–50	19
51–60	14
61–70	1

b 34

1.4 Averages and comparing data

Purposeful practice 1

1 a 4 **b** 5 **c** 5 **d** 5 **e** 6 **f** 7

2 a 1.6 **b** 1.8 **c** 2 **d** 2.2 **e** 2.4

3 a The mean decreases **b** The mean increases

4 a 8

  b **i** Mean decreases   **ii** Mean increases
    iii Mean decreases   **iv** Mean stays the same
     v Mean increases   **vi** Mean increases

Purposeful practice 2

1 a 3 **b** 6 **c** 15 **d** 5 **e** 10
  f 1.5 **g** 1 **h** 0.5

2 a 4 **b** 8 **c** 5 **d** 2 **e** 20
  f 40 **g** 80

3 a 50 **b** 40 **c** 20 **d** 70 **e** 170
  f 250 **g** 400

Problem-solving practice

1 a 9 **b** 6 **c** 3

2 a 1.6

  b The mean for the 11 numbers will be greater than the mean for the first 10 numbers as 3 is higher than the mean of 1.6

3 9

4 10

5 11 680 megabytes

1.5 Line graphs and more bar charts

Purposeful practice 1

1

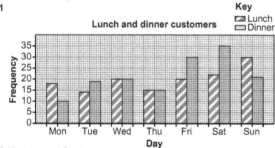

Lunch and dinner customers

2 Monday and Sunday

3 Tuesday, Friday and Saturday

4 Wednesday and Thursday

5 Saturday (57)

Purposeful practice 2

1 Monday 7 dogs and 3 cats; Tuesday 5 dogs and 5 cats; Wednesday 3 dogs and 7 cats; Thursday 4 dogs and 4 cats; Friday 3 dogs and 1 cat

2 Tuesday and Thursday

3

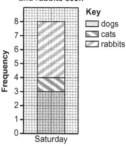

Number of dogs, cats and rabbits seen

Problem-solving practice

1 Yes, Emily is right as she sent a total of 132 text messages and Toby sent 66 text messages.

2

	Fan A	Fan B	Fan C	Fan D
Number of matches at home	22	22	16	19
Number of matches away	4	7	10	4

3 Examples of suitable diagrams:

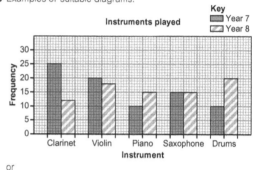

Instruments played

or

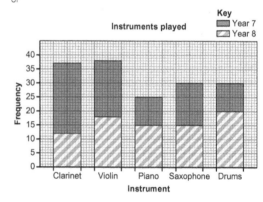

Instruments played

2.1 Mental maths

Purposeful practice 1

1 120 **2** 120 **3** 1200
4 1200 **5** 1200 **6** 1200
7 2400 **8** 2400 **9** 2400

Purposeful practice 2

1 140 **2** 28 **3** 168
4 144 **5** 48 **6** 168
7 420 **8** 312 **9** 600

Purposeful practice 3

1 20 **2** 32 **3** 50 **4** 96
5 6 **6** 1 **7** 6 **8** 10
9 5 **10** 4 **11** 24 **12** 1.5

Problem-solving practice

1 a Grace has worked out 3 × 4 and then added 2 to give 14 and then multiplied by 10. She should have worked out 3 × 4 and then 2 × 10 and then added the answers together.
  b 32
2 58p × 100 = 5800p = £58, so yes, £60 is enough
3 39, one example of the calculation is 6 + 9 × 2 + 5 × 3
4 £6, one example of the calculation is £4 × 12 − £42
5 40 × 8p + 50 × 3p = 470p = £4.70
6 0, one example of the calculation is 8 × 60 − 12 × 40
7 6 × 30 − 17 = 163
8 Abi and Bella are correct. Cameron has only added on the booking fee for one ticket, not all 3. Bella has correctly worked out the cost of 3 tickets and 3 booking fees and added them together. Abi has worked out the total cost of one ticket and the booking fee and has then worked out the total cost of all 3.
9 (4 + 3) × (8 − 6) ÷ 2

2.2 Addition and subtraction

Purposeful practice 1

1 a 593	b 594	c 594
d 603	e 613	f 623
g 723	h 823	i 923
2 a 215	b 216	c 215
d 206	e 196	f 206
g 106	h 6	i 96

Purposeful practice 2

1 a 597	b 384	c 213
2 a 1929	b 655	c 1274
3 a 223	b 713	c 713

Purposeful practice 3

1 a 100	b 100		
2 a 980	b 1000	c 1000	
3 a 9980	b 10000	c 10000	d 10000
4 a 39980	b 40000	c 40000	d 40000

Problem-solving practice

1 a 542 rounds to 500 and 173 rounds to 200. 500 + 200 = 700, Farrah's answer is closer to 600.
  b Farrah hasn't added on the 100 that she has carried over.
  c 715
2 684 − 357 = 1041 is incorrect. Alan has swapped the 357 and 684 around but also changed the + to −. Changing the order of numbers in an addition doesn't change the answer so the sign shouldn't have changed.
3 a 132 + 219 = 351 b 219 − 132 = 87
4

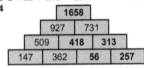

1658			
927	731		
509	418	313	
147	362	56	257

5 a
```
   4 [7] 5
+ [2] 3  6
----------
   7  1 [1]
```
b
```
   8  5 [0]
−  3 [2] 7
----------
  [5] 2  3
```

2.3 Multiplication

Purposeful practice 1

1 939	2 942	3 945
4 1368	5 1372	6 1376
7 3095	8 3100	9 3105

Purposeful practice 2

1 1064	2 1057	3 1050
4 2886	5 2880	6 2874
7 2395	8 1916	9 3353

Purposeful practice 3

1 a 496	b 4960	c 5456	d 1116
e 5022	f 468	g 2106	
2 a 1272	b 4452	c 13038	
d 11590	e 34770	f 118218	

Problem-solving practice

1 £756
```
     4 2
   × 1 8
   -----
   3 3₁6
 + 4 2 0
   -----
   7 5 6
```
2 Yes, as 16 × 28 = £448
3 a Jordan is incorrect because it isn't just one more; it's 1 × 6 more.
  b 2748
4 No, because 52 × 14 = 728
5 Job A: 24 × 15 = £360, Job B: 28 × 13 = £364 so Job B pays more.
6 27 × 36 = 972, 972 − 25 = 947 packets of sweets
7
```
    4 3 7
 ×     [8]
 ---------
 [3]4 9 6
    2 5
```

2.4 Division

Purposeful practice 1

1 a 33	b 33	c 3
2 a 27	b 27	c 8
3 a 516	b 516	c 7

Purposeful practice 2

1 a 31	b 33	c 330
d 273	e 28	f 279
g 281	h 24	i 27
2 a 16 remainder 1		b 23 remainder 1
c 35 remainder 2		d 12 remainder 3
e 25 remainder 5		f 28 remainder 4
g 22 remainder 2		h 29 remainder 12
i 36 remainder 25		

Problem-solving practice

1 136 ÷ 17 = 2312 is incorrect, because Harriet has just changed the × to ÷
2 Tariq has written 3 remainder 32 instead of 32 remainder 3.
3 £1235 ÷ 19 = £65
4
```
      33
    -----
 15 ) 500
     −45  ← 3 × 15
     ---
      50
     −45  ← 3 × 15
     ---
       5
```
So 33 full boxes
5 £14500 − £1900 = £12600, £12600 ÷ 24 = £525 each month
6 325 ÷ 22 = 14 remainder 17 so not enough flour for 15 cupcakes or 325 ÷ 15 = 21 remainder 10 so not enough flour for 15 cupcakes
7 a 172.5 b 57.5 c 218

2.5 Money and time

Purposeful practice 1

1 a £7	b £8	c £8	d £7
e £75	f £76	g £75	h £107
2 a £12.40	b £12.41	c £12.41	d £12.48
e £12.48	f £12.48	g £102.09	h £102.10

Purposeful practice 2

1 a £2	b £1.99	2 a £2	b £2.00
3 a £3	b £2.99	4 a £3	b £3.00
5 a £100	b £99.99	6 a £100	b £100.00

Purposeful practice 3

1

Time (decimal of an hour)	0	0.2	0.5	**0.75**	1
Time (fraction of an hour)	0	$\frac{1}{5}$	$\frac{1}{2}$	$\frac{3}{4}$	1
Time (minutes)	0	**12**	30	**45**	**60**

2 1 hour 15 minutes and 1.25, 4 hours 45 minutes and 4.75, 15 hours 30 minutes and 15.5, 25 hours 30 minutes and 25.5,

1 hour 45 minutes and 1.75, 25 hours 45 minutes and 25.75, 25 hours 15 minutes and 25.25, 15 hours 15 minutes and 15.25

3 a 2.25 hours   **b** 2.75 hours   **c** 4.5 hours
    d 32.25 hours   **e** 42.5 hours

Problem-solving practice

1 a Pete is wrong because he hasn't looked at the number after the pence which is 8, not 1.
    b £42.37
2 a Erin is wrong because 3.5 is $3\frac{1}{2}$ hours because $0.5 = \frac{1}{2}$
    b 3 hours 30 minutes
3 a 45 minutes is $\frac{45}{60}$ but 0.45 is $\frac{45}{100}$ so $1\frac{3}{4}$ hours is not 1.45.
    b 1.75
4 £166 + £136 + £347 + £37 + £16 = £702
5 a 3 hours 15 minutes   **b** 3.25 hours

2.6 Negative numbers

Purposeful practice 1

1 a 2   **b** −1   **c** −1
    d −2   **e** −9   **f** −20
2 a >   **b** >   **c** <   **d** <
    e >   **f** >   **g** >   **h** <
    i <   **j** >   **k** >   **l** <

Purposeful practice 2

1 a 2   **b** 1   **c** 0   **d** −1
    e −2   **f** −3   **g** −4   **h** −5
    i −6   **j** −7   **k** −8   **l** −9
2 a −2   **b** −1   **c** 0   **d** 1
    e 2   **f** 3   **g** −1   **h** 0
    i −4   **j** −3   **k** −20   **l** −21
3 a C, F, J, K   **b** A, H   **c** B, D, E, G, I, L
4 a negative   **b** positive   **c** negative
    d negative   **e** negative   **f** positive
    g negative   **h** negative   **i** negative

Problem-solving practice

1 −10, −6, −3, 1, 5
2 a Gavin has worked out 5 + 3, not −5 + 3. Jason has worked out −3 + 5, not −5 + 3.
    b −2
3 a 4°C
    b −8°C
4 a Thursday   **b** −14 °C   **c** Thursday
5 a, b Possible solutions: 2 − 8 = 4 + −10, 2 − 8 = −10 + 4,
    2 − 4 = 8 + −10, 2 − 4 = −10 + 8, 2 − −10 = 4 + 8
6 Students give any two numbers that total −5, for example 1 and −6

2.7 Factors, multiples and primes

Purposeful practice 1

1 a 1, 2   **b** 1, 2, 4
    c 1, 2, 4, 8   **d** 1, 2, 4, 8, 16
    e 1, 2, 4, 8, 16, 32   **f** 1, 2, 4, 8, 16, 32, 64
    g 1, 7   **h** 1, 2, 7, 14
    i 1, 2, 4, 7, 14, 28   **j** 1, 2, 4, 7, 8, 14, 28, 56
2 a 5, 10, 15, 20, 25, 30   **b** 15, 30, 45, 60, 75, 90
    c 25, 50, 75, 100, 125, 150   **d** 50, 100, 150, 200, 250, 300
    e 75, 150, 225, 300, 375, 450 **f** 150, 300, 450, 600, 750, 900

Purposeful practice 2

1 2   **2** 4   **3** 4
4 4   **5** 1   **6** 8
7 2   **8** 1   **9** 8

Purposeful practice 3

1 15   **2** 25   **3** 55
4 60   **5** 50   **6** 75
7 150   **8** 75   **9** 300

Problem-solving practice

1 Abdul has included the number 5, which isn't a factor of 12, and he has missed 12 from the list.
2 Chris has missed the first multiple of 7 off the list which is 7.
3 5 and 15   **4** 33   **5** 4 and 6

6 a 6, 12, 30 or 60   **b** 1, 2, 3 or 6
    c 28 or 56 or 84 or 112 and so on
7 The multiples of any even number, for example the multiples of 2 are 2, 4, 6, 8, 10, 12, ...
8 For example, 12 and 24
9 2 and 4
10 a Jacinta has worked out the highest common factor.
     b 60
11 a Students give two numbers that have a highest common factor of 40, for example, 40 and 80
     b Students give two numbers that have a lowest common multiple of 40, for example, 5 and 8

2.8 Square numbers

Purposeful practice 1

1 a 1   **b** 4   **c** 9   **d** 16
    e 25   **f** 36   **g** 49   **h** 64
    i 81   **j** 100   **k** 121   **l** 144
2 a 4   **b** 36   **c** 64   **d** 121

Purposeful practice 2

1 7   **2** 4   **3** 12   **4** 6   **5** 8
6 1   **7** 5   **8** 10   **9** 11   **10** 9

Purposeful practice 3

1 a 28   **b** 34   **c** 64   **d** 77   **e** 65
    f 25   **g** 27   **h** 9   **i** 9
2 a 19   **b** 4   **c** 16   **d** 7   **e** 28
    f 7   **g** 100   **h** 28   **i** 4

Problem-solving practice

1 a 5   **b** 7   **c** 11
    d 4   **e** 64   **f** 81
2 $\sqrt{81}$, 3^2 and 9
3 a 1 and 9   **b** 4 and 16   **c** 6 is not a square number
4 No, because 55 is not a square number; 49 is 7^2 and 64 is 8^2 so there isn't an integer square number between 49 and 64.
5 a 9(9 by 9 square using 81 tiles)   **b** 9 tiles
6 a 9   **b** 9   **c** 4
    d 3   **e** 4   **f** 5
7 3 and 4   **8** 12 and 13   **9** 6 and 8

3 Expressions, functions and formulae answers

3.1 Functions

Purposeful practice 1

1 a 16   **b** 48   **c** 8   **d** 3
2 a − 10, ÷ 2   **b** + 10, × 2   **c** − 20, ÷ 3
    d + 20, × 3   **e** − 25, ÷ 6   **f** + 15, × 4
3 a − 10   **b** × 2   **c** ÷ 3   **d** + 15

Purposeful practice 2

1 6, 10, 16   **2** 10, 14, 20   **3** 6, 14, 26   **4** 12, 20, 32
5 8, 9, 10   **6** 6, 7, 8   **7** 0, 1, 2   **8** 2, 3, 4

Problem-solving practice

1 a Jill is wrong because +10 only works for 5 + 10 = 15. It does not work for 7 → 21.
    b ×3
2 a 2 → 8
    b 8 → 4
3 Abi is correct as 8 ÷ 4 = 2, 20 ÷ 4 = 5 and 60 ÷ 4 = 15.
James is not correct as 8 − 6 = 2 but 20 − 6 ≠ 5 and 60 − 6 ≠ 15.
Sanjeev is correct as $\frac{1}{4}$ of 8 = 2, $\frac{1}{4}$ of 20 = 5 and $\frac{1}{4}$ of 60 = 15.
4

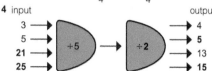

Students may have different examples for the last line.

3.2 Simplifying expressions 1

Purposeful practice 1

1 a $2x$ **b** $3x$ **c** $3x$ **d** $3x$
   e $4x$ **f** $4x$ **g** $4x$ **h** $5x$
   i $6x$ **j** $6x$ **k** $7x$ **l** $7x$

2 a 0 **b** x **c** $2x$ **d** x
   e 0 **f** x **g** $2x$ **h** $3x$

3 a -1 **b** -2 **c** -3 **d** -4
   e -3 **f** -2 **g** -1 **h** 0

4 a $-x$ **b** $-2x$ **c** $-3x$ **d** $-4x$
   e $-3x$ **f** $-2x$ **g** $-x$ **h** 0

Purposeful practice 2

1 a $2x + 3$ **b** $2x + 3$ **c** $2x + 3$ **d** $3x + 3$
   e $3x + 3$ **f** $3x + 3$ **g** $3x + 9$ **h** $3x + 9$
   i $3x + 9$

2 a $2y + 1$ **b** $2y + 1$ **c** $2y + 1$ **d** $2y + 2$
   e $2y + 2$ **f** $2y + 2$ **g** $5y - 1$ **h** $5y - 1$
   i $5y - 1$

3 a $7t + 4$ **b** $7t + 4$ **c** $7t + 4$
   d $7t + 2$ **e** $7t + 2$ **f** $7t + 2$

4 a $7a + 4b$ **b** $7a + 4b$ **c** $7a + 4b$
   d $7a + 2b$ **e** $5a + 4b$ **f** $6a + 3b$

5 a $-2c + 6$ or $6 - 2c$ **b** $-2c + 6$ or $6 - 2c$
   c $-2c + 6$ or $6 - 2c$ **d** $-2c + 6d$ or $6d - 2c$
   e $-2c + 6d$ or $6d - 2c$ **f** $-2c + 6d$ or $6d - 2c$

Problem-solving practice

1 Students give three different expressions that simplify to $12x$, for example $x + 11x$, $14x - 2x$, $5x + 8x - x$

2

13n	9n	8n
5n	**10n**	**15n**
12n	11n	7n

3 $6x + 2x$ and $10x - 2x$

4

	18a	
8a		**10a**
3a	**5a**	**5a**
a	2a	3a	2a

5 Alex is correct as you use the sign directly before the term which is $-$ for $5x$.

6

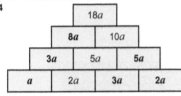

	9a + 10b	
4a + 6b		**5a + 4b**
a + 3b	3a + 3b	2a + b
b	a + 2b	2a + b	0

3.3 Simplifying expressions 2

Purposeful practice 1

1 a x **b** $2x$ **c** $3x$ **d** $5x$
   e $4x$ **f** $3x$ **g** nx **h** xy

2 a $2y$ **b** $4y$ **c** $6y$ **d** $10y$
   e $8y$ **f** $6y$ **g** $4y$ **h** $2y$

3 a ab **b** bc **c** cd **d** de
   e de **f** cd **g** bc **h** ab

4 a p^2 **b** q^2 **c** r^2 **d** s^2

Purposeful practice 2

1 a $2x + 2$ **b** $2x + 4$ **c** $2x + 6$ **d** $2x + 8$

2 a $3x + 3$ **b** $3x + 6$ **c** $3x + 9$ **d** $3x + 12$

3 a $4y + 4$ **b** $4y + 8$ **c** $4y + 12$ **d** $4y + 16$

4 a $2x - 2$ **b** $2x - 4$ **c** $2x - 6$ **d** $2x - 8$

5 a $3x - 3$ **b** $3x - 6$ **c** $3x - 9$ **d** $3x - 12$

6 a $4y - 4$ **b** $4y - 8$ **c** $4y - 12$ **d** $4y - 16$

7 a $6x + 3$ **b** $6x + 6$ **c** $6x + 15$ **d** $6x + 30$
   e $6x - 3$ **f** $6x - 6$ **g** $6x - 15$ **h** $6x - 30$

8 a $20y + 4$ **b** $20y + 8$ **c** $20y + 12$ **d** $20y + 40$
   e $20y - 4$ **f** $20y - 8$ **g** $20y - 12$ **h** $20y - 40$

Problem-solving practice

1

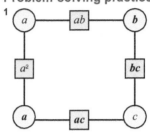

2 Students should give 2 multiplication calculations that give the answer $12n$, for example $2 \times 6n$ and $12 \times n$

3

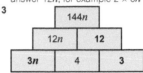

	144n	
12n		12
3n	4	3

4 $n \times n = n^2$

5 a Kevin hasn't multiplied the 5 inside the brackets by 3.
   b Jason has added 3 to both the 4 and 5 inside the brackets, instead of multiplying them.
   c $12y + 15$

6 $3(4x - 3) = 12x - 9$,
$4(x - 3) = 4x - 12$,
$3(x - 4) = 3x - 12$,
$4(x + 3) = 4x + 12$,
$4(3x + 4) = 12x + 16$,
$3(4x + 3) = 12x + 9$,
$3(x + 4) = 3x + 12$,
$4(3x - 4) = 12x - 16$.

7 a 21 **b** 3 **c** 4 and $10b$

3.4 Writing expressions

Purposeful practice 1

1 a $x + 2$ **b** $x - 2$ **c** $2x$
   d $2x$ **e** $2x$ **f** $\frac{x}{2}$

2 a $x - 3$ **b** $3x$ **c** $x + 3$
   d $\frac{x}{3}$ **e** $3 - x$ **f** $3 + x$

3 a $4x$ **b** $4 + x$ **c** $x - 4$
   d $4x$ **e** $\frac{x}{4}$ **f** $4x$

4 a $x + 5$ **b** $5 - x$ **c** $x - 5$
   d $5x$ **e** $5 - x$ **f** $\frac{x}{5}$

Purposeful practice 2

1 a 11 **b** 10 **c** 17 **d** 15

2 a 7 **b** 4 **c** 7 **d** 7

3 a 18 **b** 21 **c** 60 **d** 44

4 a $2x + 9$ **b** $3x + 7$ **c** $12x + 5$ **d** $11x + 4$

5 a $2x - 9$ or $9 - 2x$ **b** $3x - 7$ or $7 - 3x$
   c $12x - 5$ or $5 - 12x$ **d** $11x - 4$ or $4 - 11x$

6 a $18x$ **b** $21x$ **c** $60x$ **d** $44x$

7 a $11x$ **b** $10x$ **c** $17x$ **d** $15x$

8 a $7x$ **b** $4x$ **c** $7x$ **d** $7x$

Problem-solving practice

1 10 more than n and $n + 10$; 10 less than n and $n - 10$; n subtracted from 10 and $10 - n$; 10 lots of n and $10n$

2 $80 - s$

3 $\frac{y}{2}$

4 C: $y + 8$

5 a Finn has added 3 on instead of subtracting, as he's 3 years younger than Evie, not 3 years older
   b $2y - 3$

6 a Katie: p, Daniel: $2p$, Ellie: $p + 5$ **b** $4p + 5$

7 $2n + 12$

3.5 Substituting into formulae

Purposeful practice 1

1 a $A = 12, B = 9, C = 2, D = 20, E = 60, F = 5$
 b $A = 4, B = 1, C = 10, D = 4, E = 12, F = 1$
 c $A = 5, B = 2, C = 9, D = 6, E = 18, F = 1\frac{1}{2}$ or 1.5
2 a $G = 4, H = 2, I = 15, J = 3, K = 1, L = 3$
 b $G = 9, H = 3, I = 30, J = 18, K = 2, L = 2$
 c $G = 16, H = 8, I = 60, J = 48, K = 4, L = 3$
 d $G = 2, H = -2, I = 0, J = 0, K = 0, L = 0$

Purposeful practice 2

1 $M = 120, P = 50, Q = 30, R = 50, S = 70, T = 80, U = 50,$
 $V = 90, W = 107$
2 $a = 12, b = 18, c = 30, d = 34, e = 40, f = 28, g = 22, h = 30$
3 $i = 8, j = 16, k = 4, l = 20, m = 20, n = 40$
4 $p = 9, q = 16, r = 19, s = 25, t = 17, u = 41, v = 29, w = 11$

Problem-solving practice

1 a Malik has forgotten that $5a = 5 \times a$ and $3b = 3 \times b$.
 b $x = 5 \times 7 - 3 \times 2 = 29$
2 a Nick has got the priority of operations wrong; you need to do the multiplications before you add $40 + 21$
 b 61
3 $y = 23$ **4** 50 km/h **5** 80 cm²
6 a True as $P = 3 \times 6 - 2 \times 5 = 8$ and 8 is even.
 b False as $P = 3 \times 5 - 2 \times 0 = 15$ and 15 is positive.
 c True as $P = 3 \times 0 - 2 \times 5 = -10$ and -10 is negative.
 d False as $P = 3 \times 1 - 2 \times 0 = 3$ and 3 is odd. Students may have used other values of a and b to give an odd P.
 e False as $P = 3 \times 20 - 2 \times 1 = 58$ and $58 > 50$. Students may have used other values of a and b to give $P > 50$.
7 a $X = 5p - 20q$ gives the greatest value.
 b $X = pq, X = 100q$ and $X = \frac{q}{p}$ all give $X = 0$. $X = p + q$ and $X = p - q$ both give $X = 10$.
8 $A = x + y, A = x - y, A = 4x + 6y$

3.6 Writing formulae

Purposeful practice 1

1 a i $d = 7 \times 1 = 7$ **ii** $d = 7 \times 3 = 21$
 b $d = 7 \times w = 7w$
2 a i $w = \frac{14}{7} = 2$ **ii** $w = \frac{56}{7} = 8$
 b $w = \frac{d}{7}$
3 a i $m = 5 \times 60 = 300$ **ii** $m = 10 \times 60 = 600$
 b $m = x \times 60 = 60x$
4 a i $h = \frac{120}{60} = 2$ **ii** $h = \frac{240}{60} = 4$
 b $h = \frac{t}{60}$
5 a 2 is missing from each box, so $L = 2h$
 b $L = 4c$ **c** $L = 6a$ **d** $L = 8s$
 Accept letters that differ to c, a and s, as long as the three letters are different from each other.

Purposeful practice 2

1 a $L = 2x + 4$ **b** $L = 2x + 4y$
 c $L = 2x + 4z$ **d** $L = 6 + 4z$
 e $L = 6 + 8z$ **f** $L = 6n + 8z$
 g $L = 8z + 2$ **h** $L = 8z + 6f$
 i $L = 8z + 6g$ **j** $L = 4k + 6g$
2 a $P = T + C$ **b** $P = 2T$
 c $P = 3C$ **d** $P = 2T + C$
 e $P = 2T + 3C$ **f** $P = 4T + C$
 g $P = 3T + C$ **h** $P = 2T + 1$
 i $P = 2T + 2$ **j** $P = 3C - 1$
 k $P = 3C - 2$ **l** $P = 2T - 1$

Problem-solving practice

1 $L = 4x + 7$
2 Student A is correct. Student B is wrong as their formula is for 3 teas and 2 cookies (variables are the wrong way round). Student C is wrong as they have subtracted a £1 tip, not added.
3 $A = 4s + 3c + 80$ Accept a different letter to A.

4 a $T = 8b + 3p$ **b** $C = 8X + 3Y$
 Accept letters that differ from T and Y.
5 a $M = 400s + 750l$ **b** $G = 400a + 750b + 250$
 Accept letters that differ from M and G.

Mixed exercises A

Mixed problem-solving practice A

1 a £112   **b** Jeans and shirt
2 a Multiples of 3: 1. Factors of 36: 15 and 16. Square numbers: 2 and 8
 b 1 and 2 should be in factors of 36;
 15 should be in multiples of 3;
 1 and 16 should be in square numbers
3 a £60   **b** £243   **c** 32 hours
4 a   **b** $+3$

input	output
1	1
4	13
7	25
9	33

5 a C, Q   **b** A, S   **c** D, R   **d** B, P
6 30 boxes, as $9000 \div 12 = 750$, and $750 \div 25 = 30$
7 a 1, 5, 5 or 5, 5, 9. Two of the numbers must be 5, as the mode is 5, and the other number is either 4 lower or 4 higher than 5 to give the range of 4.
 b 11, 13, 14, 14. Two numbers must be either side of 13.5 and average to 13.5. The larger number cannot be greater than 14 (so it must be 14), and so the smaller number must be 13.
 c There have to be two 5s (there cannot be three 5s as the median wouldn't be 8), the middle number has to be 8, and the total of the five numbers is 50. So the total of the remaining two numbers is 32. They cannot be less than 8 and they cannot both be 16, as this would change the mode. So there are many different possible answers, for example, 5, 5, 8, 15, 17 or 5, 5, 8, 9, 23.
 d All three numbers total 0, so the two numbers must add to make -5, for example -5, 0, 5
8 a Montana: $18 + 14 + 12 + 17 + 19 = 80$.
 Lexi: $13 + 11 + 8 + 14 + 21 = 67$. Montana sent more.
 b

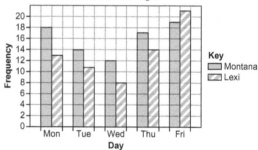

 c Friday
9 No, as $T = 12x + 5y$. It's likely that Zara has combined the two terms by adding 12 and 5 and multiplying x and y, but this cannot be done without affecting the answer.

4 Decimals and measures

4.1 Decimals and rounding

Purposeful practice 1

1 a 2 tens   **b** 2 tens   **c** 2 units   **d** 2 tenths
 e 2 hundredths **f** 2 tenths **g** 2 hundredths **h** 2 thousandths

Purposeful practice 2

1 a 17   **b** 16.7   **2 a** 17   **b** 16.6
3 a 16   **b** 16.5   **4 a** 16   **b** 16.1
5 a 16   **b** 16.0   **6 a** 16   **b** 15.9
7 a 16   **b** 15.6   **8 a** 15   **b** 15.5
9 a 15   **b** 15.1   **10 a** 15   **b** 15.0

Purposeful practice 3

1 a 18	**b** 18	**c** 27
d 27	**e** 30	**f** 30
g 20	**h** 18	**i** 36
2 a 18	**b** 12	**c** 6
d 40	**e** 25	**f** 50
g 12	**h** 7	**i** 30
j 5	**k** 51 allow 50	**l** 7

Problem-solving practice

1 a Alex has taken the digits 99 and rounded them up to 100, but has not carried the 1 to round the 7 up to 8.

   b 8

2 No, it is 7 hundredths, not 7 hundreds, as it is in the $\frac{1}{100}$ s column.

3 23.96 and 24.03

4 Students' answers must round to 10 when rounding to the nearest whole number and they must also round to 10 when rounding to the nearest 1 d.p., for example, 9.95

5 a Will has rounded 4.09 to 5 instead of 4.

   b Zannah has used his calculator and has not rounded 4.09 and 7.8 first.

   c 32

6 Mohamed gave a better estimate as he has rounded 36.5 to the nearest number that is divisible by 4.

4.2 Length, mass and capacity

Purposeful practice 1

1 a 6	**b** 60	**c** 600	**d** 0.6
e 6	**f** 60	**g** 6.5	**h** 65
i 650	**j** 6.05	**k** 0.65	**l** 600.5
2 a 705	**b** 70.5	**c** 7.05	**d** 96.1
e 9.61	**f** 0.961	**g** 3.8	**h** 0.38
i 0.038	**j** 0.17	**k** 0.017	**l** 0.00017

Purposeful practice 2

1 a 220 mm	**b** 2.2 cm	**c** 2020 mm	**d** 20.2 cm
e 2.02 m	**f** 20 200 cm	**g** 0.2 km	**h** 200 000 m
i 2.002 kg	**j** 22 000 g	**k** 0.02 litres	**l** 20 000 ml
2 a >	**b** <	**c** >	**d** >	**e** <

Problem-solving practice

1 a Li has divided by 10, not multiplied by 10.

   b 47

2 Pete has not converted the units to the same unit, for example, 6.5 cm = 65 mm, which is greater than 63 mm.

3 No, as 1550 mm = 155 cm, which is less than 160 cm

4 Zara is incorrect as 42 km = 42 000 m, so they have both travelled the same distance.

5 10 litres = 10 000 ml, 10 000 ÷ 500 = 20 times

6 2000 ÷ 250 = 8 glasses

7 Burj Khalifa and Shangai Tower

4.3 Scales and measures

Purposeful practice 1

1 a 30	**b** 20	**c** 45
d 20	**e** 12	**f** 25
2 a 40 ml	**b** 175 g	**c** 325 cm
d 5 mm	**e** 50 cm	**f** 175 cm
g 1600 m	**h** 1600 g	**i** 1600 ml

Purposeful practice 2

1 4 cm 2 mm	**2** 4 cm 3 mm	**3** 4 m 20 cm
4 4 m 30 cm	**5** 4 m 31 cm	**6** 4 m 32 cm
7 4 km 300 m	**8** 4 km 350 m	**9** 4 km 358 m

Problem-solving practice

1 a Jo is incorrect because there are 5 divisions from 0 to 10, so each division is 2 units.

   b 4

2 A is 5.8, B is 5, C is 6 and D is 5.7 so the smallest value is B.

3 A is 105 cm, B is 1.1 m = 110 cm, C is 1.2 m = 120 cm and D is 100 cm so the longest length is C.

4 a 0.2 m is not 2 cm

   b 4 m 20 cm

5 Neil is correct as 1000 m = 1 km, so 0.25 km = 250 m (0.25 × 1000 = 250)

6 Yes, it will as 1.2 cm = 1 m 20 cm and the stick is shorter than this.

4.4 Working with decimals mentally

Purposeful practice 1

1 a 0.8	**b** 0.08	**c** 0.08
d 0.8	**e** 0.08	**f** 0.08
g 2.4	**h** 0.24	**i** 0.24
j 2.4	**k** 0.24	**l** 0.24
2 a 6	**b** 0.06	**c** 0.06
d 0.6	**e** 0.06	**f** 0.6

Purposeful practice 2

1 39	**2** 41.6	**3** 77	**4** 85.8
5 102	**6** 132.6	**7** 248	**8** 260.4

Purposeful practice 3

1 a 170.4	**b** 1.704	**c** 170.4
d 17.04	**e** 1704	**f** 17 040
2 a 28.8	**b** 0.288	**c** 0.288
d 28.8	**e** 2.88	**f** 28.8

Problem-solving practice

1 a Luca may have worked out 0.3 = 3 ÷ 10 and 0.1 = 1 ÷ 10, so 0.3 × 0.1 = 3 ÷ 10 × 1 ÷ 10 = 3 ÷ 100, but then he may have incorrectly worked out 3 ÷ 100 as 0.3

   b 0.03

2 Hannah is correct, as 0.5 = 5 ÷ 10 and 0.6 = 6 ÷ 10 so 0.5 × 0.6 = 5 ÷ 10 × 6 ÷ 10 = 30 ÷ 100 = 0.30 = 0.3

3 a This is wrong. Only one 1.1 has been added to 44 and not three 1.1s. The correct answer is 47.3

   b This is correct. 32 has been correctly partitioned and both 30 and 2 have been multiplied by 1.4

4 No. 670 is 100 times more than 6.7 but 0.48 is 10 times smaller than 4.8, so overall the answer to 670 × 0.48 should be 10 times more than the answer to 6.7 × 4.8

5 a Correct	**b** Incorrect	**c** Correct
d Correct	**e** Correct	**f** Incorrect
6 a 0.06	**b** 0.58	**c** 0.348
d 6	**e** 58	**f** 0.58

7 Any five calculations relating to 4.2 × 0.7 = 2.94, for example, 42 × 0.7 = 29.4, 4.2 × 7 = 29.4, 42 × 0.07 = 2.94, 0.42 × 7 = 2.94 and 0.42 × 0.7 = 0.294

8 0.19 × 73, 19 × 0.73, 0.019 × 730

9 Any four calculations relating to 3.8 × 2.4, for example, 38 × 0.24, 0.38 × 24, 380 × 0.024 and 0.038 × 240

4.5 Working with decimals

Purposeful practice 1

1 a 5.9	**b** 6	**c** 6.1	
d 5.1	**e** 5	**f** 4.9	
2 a 6.9	**b** 7	**c** 7.1	**d** 8.1
e 10.1	**f** 11.2	**g** 6.1	**h** 6
i 5.9	**j** 4.9	**k** 5	**l** 4.9
3 a 5	**b** 8	**c** 9	**d** 4
e 6	**f** 3	**g** 10	**h** 9
4 a 3.8	**b** 4.3	**c** 2.6	**d** 1.5
e 4.4	**f** 1.3	**g** 6.2	**h** 4.1

Purposeful practice 2

1 a 55.79	**b** 25.9	**c** 33.87
d 33.88	**e** 33.881	**f** 33.576
2 a 31.02	**b** 49.02	**c** 47.87
d 47.82	**e** 47.889	**f** 47.819

Purposeful practice 3

1 a 21.6	**b** 8.1	**c** 22.4	
d 8.61	**e** 216.39		
2 a 13.4	**b** 5.8	**c** 46.2	**d** 24.67

Problem-solving practice

1 6.1 m	**2** 1.9 km	**3** 35.6 litres

4 a Wendy has not lined up the decimal point or the ones with the ones and tenths with tenths.

   b 41.58

5 6.8 kg   **6** 5.4 m   **7** £14.56

8 a Grace has not carried the 4 ones to the two tenths.
  b 10.7

4.6 Perimeter

Purposeful practice 1

1 46 mm   **2** 34 mm   **3** 70 mm
4 54 mm   **5** 54 mm   **6** 62 mm

Purposeful practice 2

1 12 cm   **2** 16 cm   **3** 20 cm   **4** 24 cm
5 24 cm   **6** 32 cm   **7** 40 cm   **8** 48 cm

Purposeful practice 3

1 $4a$ cm   **2** $4a + 2$ cm   **3** $4a + 4$ cm
4 $4a + 6$ cm   **5** $4a + 8$ cm   **6** $4a + 10$ cm

Problem-solving practice

1 5 cm   **2** 6 cm

3 a 36 cm
  b Perimeter of rectangle = 8 + 10 + 8 + 10 = 36 cm
   Perimeter of shape = 8 + 10 + 5 + 3 + 3 + 7 = 36 cm
   The two perimeters are equal because the two new 3 cm
   sides cancel out the fact that two sides of the rectangle were
   reduced in length by 3 cm.

4 a There are two sides that are not labelled that Tom has not
   included in the perimeter; they are 7 cm and 3 cm.
  b 42 cm

5 12 cm

4.7 Area

Purposeful practice 1

1 2 cm²   **2** 8 cm²   **3** 18 cm²   **4** 32 cm²

Purposeful practice 2

1 21 m²   **2** 32 m²   **3** 53 m²
4 53 m²   **5** 74 m²   **6** 50 m²

Purposeful practice 3

1 b cm²   **2** $2b$ cm²   **3** $3b$ cm²
4 $4b$ cm²   **5** $5b$ cm²

Problem-solving practice

1 7 cm

2 5 cm

3 $x = 12$

4 Students should draw three different rectangles each with an
area of 24 cm², for example 1 cm by 24 cm, 2 cm by 12 cm,
3 cm by 8 cm or 4 cm by 6 cm.

5 a Freya has worked out the area of two rectangles that overlap.
   She could have separated them out into the 12 cm by 6 cm
   and 3 cm by 5 cm rectangles, or the 9 cm by 5 cm and 6 cm by
   7 cm rectangles. Or she could have worked out the area of the
   12 cm by 9 cm rectangle and then subtracted the missing 3 cm
   by 7 cm rectangle.
  b 87 cm²

6 12 cm

4.8 More units of measure

Purposeful practice 1

1 cm³   **2** km   **3** feet   **4** hectares   **5** tonnes

Purposeful practice 2

1 7000   **2** 7100   **3** 7180   **4** 7189
5 71 890   **6** 4000   **7** 4200   **8** 4260
9 4263   **10** 42 630   **11** 93 000   **12** 93 500

Purposeful practice 3

1 a 70 000   **b** 7   **c** 3000
  d 0.03   **e** 82   **f** 82 000
2 a 1800   **b** 18   **c** 2
  d 0.2   **e** 16   **f** 20

Problem-solving practice

1 Yes, Tia is correct because 300 cm³ = 300 millilitres = 0.3 litres
2 4.2 + 0.3 = 4.5 t

3 32.5 − 0.8 = 31.7 ha

4 3 feet ≈ 90 cm, which is longer than 85 cm

5 2 feet ≈ 60 cm, 60 ÷ 2 = 30, 30 books

6 No, Yasmina is incorrect because 2 miles ≈ 3.2 km which is
further than 3 km

7 Willis Tower, Empire State Building, Bank of America Tower,
Chrysler Building
Bank of America Tower ≈ 1200 × 30 = 36 000 cm = 360 m
Willis Tower ≈ 1729 × 30 = 51 870 cm = 518.7 m

8 Yes, the truck will fit as 10 feet ≈ 10 × 30 = 300 cm = 3 m

5 Fractions and percentages

5.1 Comparing fractions

Purposeful practice 1

1 a >   **b** <   **c** >
2 a <   **b** >   **c** <   **d** <
3 a >   **b** <   **c** >   **d** <
4 a <   **b** <   **c** >   **d** <

Purposeful practice 2

1 a >   **b** >   **c** <   **d** <
  e <   **f** <   **g** >   **h** <
  i >   **j** <   **k** >   **l** >

Purposeful practice 3

1 a <   **b** >   **c** >   **d** <
  e <   **f** >   **g** <   **h** >
  i >   **j** <   **k** >   **l** >
  m <   **n** <   **o** >

Problem-solving practice

1 Mark is incorrect as $\frac{1}{5} > \frac{1}{6}$. Students may use diagrams to
explain.

2 There are more red counters, because when the numerators
are the same, the smaller denominator gives the larger fraction.
Students may use diagrams to explain.

3 a False because when denominators are equal, a larger
   numerator gives a larger fraction.
  b True because when the numerators are the same, the smaller
   denominator gives the larger fraction.
  c False because $\frac{3}{8} < \frac{2}{5}$. Students may use diagrams to explain.

4 $\frac{5}{12}$ is larger

5 Ali is incorrect, as $\frac{3}{4}$ is greater than $\frac{5}{8}$. Students may use
diagrams to explain.

6 Becky

7 Colin is incorrect, because $\frac{1}{2} < \frac{3}{5} < \frac{5}{8}$. Students may use diagrams
to explain.

5.2 Simplifying fractions

Purposeful practice 1

1 a 1   **b** 1   **c** 1   **d** 1   **e** 1   **f** 1
2 a $1\frac{1}{2}$ **b** $1\frac{1}{3}$ **c** $1\frac{1}{6}$ **d** $1\frac{1}{10}$ **e** $1\frac{1}{56}$ **f** $1\frac{1}{92}$
  g $2\frac{1}{2}$ **h** $3\frac{1}{2}$ **i** $4\frac{1}{2}$ **j** $1\frac{2}{3}$ **k** $2\frac{1}{3}$ **l** $2\frac{2}{3}$
  m $1\frac{3}{5}$ **n** $1\frac{4}{5}$ **o** $2\frac{1}{5}$ **p** $2\frac{2}{5}$ **q** $1\frac{3}{10}$ **r** $2\frac{3}{10}$

Purposeful practice 2

1 a $\frac{6}{10}, \frac{12}{20}$ **b** $\frac{12}{20}$

2 a $\frac{10}{12}, \frac{30}{36}$ **b** $\frac{30}{36}$

3 a $\frac{6}{15}, \frac{2}{5}$ **b** $\frac{4}{10}, \frac{2}{5}$ **c** $\frac{2}{5}$

4 a $\frac{7}{28}, \frac{1}{4}$ **b** $\frac{2}{8}, \frac{1}{4}$ **c** $\frac{1}{4}$

Problem-solving practice

1 Seb has the wrong denominator; the denominator should be 4.
$\frac{11}{4} = 2\frac{3}{4}$

2 Kyle and Mel are correct as ÷2 twice is the same as ÷4, but Liz
has not fully simplified the fraction.

3 a Ned divides 6 and 9 by 2, but 9 isn't divisible by 2.
He should have divided by 3, or divided 12 and 18 by 6.

b $\frac{2}{3}$

4 Natalie has started with $\frac{1}{2}$ and has then just doubled each time so she has missed fractions out. She should have started with $\frac{1}{2}$, doubled it, then started with $\frac{1}{2}$ again and tripled it, and so on, to give $\frac{1}{2}, \frac{2}{4}, \frac{3}{6}, \frac{4}{8}, \frac{5}{10}$

5 $\frac{3}{4}, \frac{6}{8}, \frac{12}{16}$ and $\frac{24}{32}$;

$\frac{1}{3}, \frac{4}{12}, \frac{5}{15}$ and $\frac{10}{30}$;

$\frac{2}{5}, \frac{4}{10}, \frac{6}{15}$ and $\frac{10}{25}$.

5.3 Working with fractions

Purposeful practice 1

1 a $\frac{2}{3}$ **b** $\frac{1}{3}$ **c** $\frac{3}{5}$ **d** $\frac{2}{5}$ **e** $\frac{4}{5}$ **f** $\frac{2}{5}$

g $\frac{4}{5}$ **h** $\frac{3}{5}$ **i** $\frac{1}{5}$ **j** $\frac{4}{7}$ **k** $\frac{1}{7}$ **l** $\frac{3}{7}$

m $\frac{6}{7}$ **n** $\frac{2}{7}$ **o** $\frac{3}{7}$

2 a $\frac{1}{2}$ **b** $\frac{1}{2}$ **c** $\frac{1}{3}$ **d** $\frac{2}{3}$ **e** $\frac{1}{4}$ **f** $\frac{1}{2}$

g $\frac{3}{4}$ **h** $\frac{1}{4}$ **i** $\frac{1}{2}$ **j** $\frac{3}{4}$ **k** $\frac{1}{3}$ **l** $\frac{2}{3}$

m $\frac{2}{3}$ **n** $\frac{1}{3}$ **o** $\frac{2}{3}$

Purposeful practice 2

1 a 2   **b** 1   **c** 3   **d** 4   **e** 5

2 a $\frac{2}{3}$ **b** $\frac{1}{3}$ **c** $\frac{1}{4}$ **d** $\frac{2}{5}$

e $\frac{1}{6}$ **f** $\frac{2}{7}$ **g** $\frac{3}{8}$ **h** $\frac{4}{9}$

Purposeful practice 3

1 a 3   **b** 4   **c** 3   **d** 6
e 5   **f** 2   **g** 2   **h** 2

2 a 8   **b** 12   **c** 4   **d** 4   **e** 9
f 18   **g** 6   **h** 6   **i** 24   **j** 8

Problem-solving practice

1 Nia is right because 5 out of the 10 squares are shaded and $\frac{1}{2}$ of $10 = 5$

2 a Jack has subtracted the numerators and the denominators; he should have only subtracted the numerators.

b $\frac{1}{5}$

3 Alex asks 100 students in total. $\frac{1}{4}$ of 100 = 25, not 30.

4 25 sweets. $\frac{1}{3}$ of 60 = 20 and $\frac{1}{4}$ of 60 = 15
$60 - (20 + 15) = 25$

5 $\frac{7}{10}$ of £80 = £56
Felix gets £80 − £56 = £24

5.4 Fractions and decimals

Purposeful practice 1

1 a $\frac{1}{10}$ **b** $\frac{1}{5}$ **c** $\frac{3}{10}$ **d** $\frac{2}{5}$ **e** $\frac{1}{2}$
f $\frac{3}{5}$ **g** $\frac{7}{10}$ **h** $\frac{4}{5}$ **i** $\frac{9}{10}$

2 a 0.2   **b** 0.4   **c** 0.6   **d** 0.8

3 a $\frac{1}{100}$ **b** $\frac{1}{50}$ **c** $\frac{3}{100}$ **d** $\frac{1}{25}$ **e** $\frac{1}{20}$
f $\frac{3}{50}$ **g** $\frac{7}{100}$ **h** $\frac{2}{25}$ **i** $\frac{9}{100}$

4 a 0.01   **b** 0.03   **c** 0.07   **d** 0.09   **e** 0.02
f 0.06   **g** 0.04   **h** 0.08   **i** 0.05

Purposeful practice 2

1 a $\frac{3}{25}$ **b** $\frac{3}{20}$ **c** $\frac{23}{100}$ **d** $\frac{1}{4}$ **e** $\frac{33}{100}$ **f** $\frac{9}{25}$

g $\frac{21}{50}$ **h** $\frac{14}{25}$ **i** $\frac{13}{20}$ **j** $\frac{18}{25}$ **k** $\frac{81}{100}$ **l** $\frac{23}{25}$

2 a 0.12   **b** 0.24   **c** 0.15   **d** 0.3
e 0.6   **f** 0.36   **g** 0.72   **h** 0.42
i 0.84   **j** 0.56   **k** 0.28

Problem-solving practice

1 Eliza has written the 1 before the decimal point and the 2 after. First Eliza needs to find a fraction equivalent to $\frac{1}{2}$ with a denominator of 10
$\frac{1}{2} = \frac{5}{10} = 0.5$

2 $\frac{65}{100} = 0.65$

3 $\frac{3}{4}$ and 0.75, $\frac{1}{2}$ and 0.5, $\frac{1}{4}$ and 0.25, $\frac{1}{5}$ and 0.2, $\frac{7}{10}$ and 0.7, $\frac{4}{5}$ and 0.8

4 $\frac{3}{10}$ because $\frac{3}{10} = 0.3$ and $\frac{3}{5} = 0.6$

5 a False, because $\frac{2}{5} = \frac{4}{10} = 0.4$

b False, because $\frac{3}{20} = \frac{15}{100} = 0.15$

c True, because $\frac{9}{25} = \frac{36}{100} = 0.36$

6 a $\frac{27}{50}$ **b** 0.54

7 0.28

8 Maddy has written the numerator 14 after the decimal point but she can't do this because the denominator is 25. First Maddy needs to find a fraction equivalent to $\frac{14}{25}$ with a denominator of 100.
$\frac{14}{25} = \frac{56}{100} = 0.56$

5.5 Understanding percentages

Purposeful practice 1

1 a 29%   **b** 52%   **c** 79%   **d** 99%
e 30%   **f** 3%   **g** 80%   **h** 8%

2 a i $\frac{10}{100}$ **ii** 10%   **b i** $\frac{30}{100}$ **ii** 30%

c i $\frac{70}{100}$ **ii** 70%   **d i** $\frac{90}{100}$ **ii** 90%

e i $\frac{2}{100}$ **ii** 2%   **f i** $\frac{18}{100}$ **ii** 18%

g i $\frac{26}{100}$ **ii** 26%   **h i** $\frac{46}{100}$ **ii** 46%

i i $\frac{72}{100}$ **ii** 72%   **j i** $\frac{82}{100}$ **ii** 82%

k i $\frac{98}{100}$ **ii** 98%   **l i** $\frac{4}{100}$ **ii** 4%

m i $\frac{28}{100}$ **ii** 28%   **n i** $\frac{44}{100}$ **ii** 44%

o i $\frac{60}{100}$ **ii** 60%   **p i** $\frac{92}{100}$ **ii** 92%

q i $\frac{5}{100}$ **ii** 5%   **r i** $\frac{45}{100}$ **ii** 45%

s i $\frac{65}{100}$ **ii** 65%   **t i** $\frac{95}{100}$ **ii** 95%

3 a i 0.1   **ii** 10%   **b i** 0.3   **ii** 30%
c i 0.7   **ii** 70%   **d i** 0.9   **ii** 90%
e i 1   **ii** 100%   **f i** 0.5   **ii** 50%
g i 0.25   **ii** 25%   **h i** 0.75   **ii** 75%
i i 0.2   **ii** 20%   **j i** 0.4   **ii** 40%
k i 0.8   **ii** 80%   **l i** 1   **ii** 100%

Purposeful practice 2

1 a 0.01   **b** 0.06   **c** 0.08   **d** 0.1   **e** 0.2
f 0.6   **g** 0.8   **h** 1   **i** 0.18   **j** 0.23
k 0.42   **l** 0.55   **m** 0.62   **n** 0.74   **o** 0.92
p 1.05   **q** 1.1   **r** 1.2

2 a 32%   **b** 30%   **c** 2%   **d** 78%
e 70%   **f** 8%   **g** 56%   **h** 50%
i 6%   **j** 93%   **k** 90%   **l** 3%
m 135%   **n** 100%   **o** 130%   **p** 105%

Problem-solving practice

1 No, because $\frac{1}{5} = \frac{20}{100} = 20\%$, not 5%

2 B 1.15

3 $\frac{3}{4}$ and 75%, $\frac{1}{2}$ and 50%, $\frac{2}{5}$ and 40%, $\frac{3}{10}$ and 30%,
$\frac{43}{50}$ and 86%, $\frac{7}{20}$ and 35%

4 30% is bigger because $\frac{1}{4} = 25\%$

5 a True because $\frac{31}{50} = \frac{62}{100} = 62\%$

   b False because $\frac{1}{20} = \frac{5}{100} = 5\%$, not 20%

   c False because $\frac{7}{10} = \frac{70}{100} = 70\%$, not 7%

6 a $\frac{29}{50}$ **b** 58%

7 45%

5.6 Percentages of amounts

Purposeful practice 1

1 a 20   **b** 6   **c** 3   **d** 4

   e 90   **f** 7   **g** 2   **h** 1

2 a 6 cm   **b** 12 cm   **c** 36 cm

   d 30 cm   **e** 3 cm   **f** 0.6 cm

3 a 1.2 kg   **b** 3.6 kg   **c** 8.4 kg

   d 6 kg   **e** 0.6 kg   **f** 0.12 kg

4 a £4.20   **b** £8.40   **c** £16.80

   d £21   **e** £2.10   **f** £0.42

Purposeful practice 2

1 a £30   **b** £3   **c** £33   **d** £60   **e** £6

   f £66   **g** £15   **h** £21   **i** £81

2 a £25   **b** £12.50   **c** £2.50

   d £37.50   **e** £15   **f** £40

   g £75   **h** £90   **i** £112.50

Purposeful practice 3

1 a 0.1   **b** 0.2   **c** 0.3   **d** 0.4   **e** 0.5

   f 0.6   **g** 0.7   **h** 0.8   **i** 0.9   **j** 0.01

2 a 100, 20   **b** 250, 50   **c** 350, 70   **d** 450, 90

Problem-solving practice

1 20% is $\frac{1}{5}$, so Jeff should have divided by 5, not 20

   20% of 320 = 64

2 a £110   **b** £2090

3 65% of 80 = 52 and 45% of 120 = 54, so 45% of 120 is the greater value

4 No, because 95% of 800 = 760

5 0.15 × 120 = 18 customers

6 15% of £60 = £9 which is a bigger discount than £8

7 A 5% pay rise is higher than £20 because 5% of £480 = £24.

8 65% of 60 minutes = 39 minutes, 42 − 39 = 3 minutes

6 Probability

6.1 The language of probability

Purposeful practice

1 a i 2   **ii** 1, 5   **iii** 3   **iv** 4   **v** 1, 2   **vi** 4

   b 1   **c i** 3, 4   **ii** 2, 3   **iii** 5

2

impossible	unlikely	even chance	likely	certain
0		0.5		1
C	A	D	E	B

3 a i U, Q, S, T   **ii** V, W, P, R

   b Q 20%, S 30%, T 40%, V 60%, W 70%, P 80%, R 90%

Problem-solving practice

1 Bag A likely, Bag B even chance, Bag C certain, Bag D impossible, Bag E unlikely

2 a A, C and D   **b** C

   c It isn't even chance with set A or B because the number of blue counters is not equal to half of the total.

   d Students draw a set of counters where half of them are blue.

3 Any event that has a probability of 0.5, for example a fair coin landing on heads.

4 Any spinner where 5 sections contain D and the other three contain A, B, C respectively.

6.2 Calculating probability

Purposeful practice 1

1 a $\frac{1}{2}$ **b** 0   **c** 1   **d** $\frac{1}{3}$ **e** $\frac{2}{3}$ **f** 0

   g 1   **h** $\frac{2}{4}$ or $\frac{1}{2}$ **i** $\frac{3}{4}$ **j** $\frac{1}{4}$

2 a $\frac{1}{2}$ **b** 0   **c** 1   **d** $\frac{1}{3}$ **e** $\frac{2}{3}$ **f** 1

   g 0   **h** $\frac{2}{4}$ or $\frac{1}{2}$ **i** $\frac{3}{4}$ **j** $\frac{1}{4}$

Purposeful practice 2

1 a P(red) = 1, P(blue) = 0   **b** P(red) = $\frac{4}{5}$, P(blue) = $\frac{1}{5}$

   c P(red) = $\frac{3}{5}$, P(blue) = $\frac{2}{5}$ **d** P(red) = $\frac{2}{5}$, P(blue) = $\frac{3}{5}$

   e P(red) = $\frac{1}{5}$, P(blue) = $\frac{4}{5}$ **f** P(red) = 0, P(blue) = 1

2 a P(red) = 1, P(blue) = 0   **b** P(red) = $\frac{3}{4}$, P(blue) = $\frac{1}{4}$

   c P(red) = $\frac{1}{2}$, P(blue) = $\frac{1}{2}$ **d** P(red) = $\frac{1}{4}$, P(blue) = $\frac{3}{4}$

   e P(red) = 0, P(blue) = 1

Problem-solving practice

1 a $\frac{1}{9}$ **b** $\frac{2}{9}$ **c** $\frac{3}{9}$ or $\frac{1}{3}$

   d No, because it depends on how many odd and even numbers are on the cards.

   e $\frac{5}{9}$

2 Yellow and red. P(yellow) = $\frac{2}{7}$ and P(red) = $\frac{2}{7}$ so the probabilities are the same.

3 a A $\frac{1}{8}$, B $\frac{3}{8}$, C $\frac{1}{2}$, D $\frac{7}{8}$, E $\frac{5}{8}$

   b Students draw an 8-sided spinner with 2 green sections.

4 $\frac{7}{12}$ **5** $\frac{17}{32}$

6.3 More probability calculations

Purposeful practice 1

1 $\frac{4}{11}$ **2** $\frac{7}{11}$ **3** $\frac{5}{11}$ **4** $\frac{6}{11}$ **5** $\frac{2}{11}$ **6** $\frac{9}{11}$

7 $\frac{9}{11}$ **8** $\frac{2}{11}$ **9** $\frac{6}{11}$ **10** $\frac{5}{11}$ **11** $\frac{7}{11}$ **12** $\frac{4}{11}$

Purposeful practice 2

2 1, certain   **3** 0.5, even chance   **4** 0.2, unlikely

5 0.7, likely   **6** 1, certain   **7** 0, impossible

8 0.5, even chance   **9** 0.8, likely   **10** 0.3, unlikely

Purposeful practice 3

1 $\frac{1}{9}$ **2** $\frac{2}{9}$ **3** $\frac{3}{9}$ or $\frac{1}{3}$ **4** $\frac{6}{9}$ or $\frac{2}{3}$

5 $\frac{5}{9}$ **6** $\frac{4}{9}$ **7** $\frac{8}{9}$ **8** $\frac{8}{9}$

9 $\frac{7}{9}$ **10** $\frac{7}{9}$ **11** $\frac{1}{9}$ **12** $\frac{3}{9}$ or $\frac{1}{3}$

Problem-solving practice

1 0.7   **2** Yes, as 1 − 65% = 100% − 65% = 35%

3 $\frac{5}{8}$ **4 a** $\frac{6}{25}$ **b** $\frac{17}{25}$ **c** 0

5 P(not R) = $\frac{5}{8}$; spinner B   P(G or R) = $\frac{7}{8}$; spinner C

   P(not Y) = $\frac{1}{8}$; spinner E   P(R or G) = $\frac{5}{8}$; spinner A

   P(R or G) = 1; spinner D

6 2 ones, 1 four and 2 other numbers from 2, 3 or 5.

6.4 Experimental probability

Purposeful practice 1

1

Result	Frequency	Experimental probability
head	56	$\frac{56}{100}$
tail	44	$\frac{44}{100}$
Total	100	

Result	Frequency	Experimental probability
6	16	$\frac{16}{150}$
not 6	**134**	$\frac{134}{150}$
Total	150	

Train arrives	Frequency	Experimental probability
on time	147	$\frac{147}{200}$
late	**53**	$\frac{53}{200}$
Total	200	

Judy arrives	Frequency	Experimental probability
early	**1**	$\frac{1}{21}$
on time	15	$\frac{15}{21}$
late	5	$\frac{5}{21}$
Total	21	

Purposeful practice 2

1 0, $\frac{7}{19}$, $\frac{4}{30}$, $\frac{11}{40}$, $\frac{8}{30}$

2 a 30 **b** 120

3 $\frac{30}{120} = \frac{1}{4}$

4 Not enough trials. On a fair dice P(6) = $\frac{1}{6}$, so getting a six on one roll is unlikely.

Problem-solving practice

1 a $\frac{5}{7}$ **b** Use more results

2 a No, because the denominator should be the total of 16 and 34, which is 50.
b Yes, as P(white) = $\frac{34}{50}$, which simplifies to $\frac{17}{25}$

3 No, because P(not 1) = $\frac{70}{80} = \frac{7}{8}$, which is more than $\frac{3}{4}$

6.5 Expected outcomes

Purposeful practice 1

1 a i $\frac{4}{5}$ **ii** $\frac{1}{5}$ **b i** 8 **ii** 2

2 a i $\frac{4}{10}$ **ii** $\frac{3}{10}$ **iii** $\frac{3}{10}$
b i 8 **ii** 6 **iii** 6

3 a i $\frac{4}{10}$ **ii** $\frac{3}{10}$ **iii** $\frac{2}{10}$ **iv** $\frac{1}{10}$
b i 12 **ii** 9 **iii** 6 **iv** 3

4 a i $\frac{1}{10}$ **ii** $\frac{2}{10}$ **iii** $\frac{3}{10}$ **iv** $\frac{4}{10}$
b i 3 **ii** 6 **iii** 9 **iv** 12

Purposeful practice 2

1 a A 6, B 4, C 8, D 3, E 6, F 9
b A 12, B 8, C 16, D 6, E 12, F 18
2 A £6 B £0 C £12 D −£3 E £6 F £15
3 a Yes
b No, it's 3, which is one less than expected.
c £9 − 12 = −£3 or £3 loss

Problem-solving practice

1 15

2 a 75 **b** 45

c No, because there aren't an equal amount of each colour; there are 2 yellow counters so the expected number is $\frac{2}{10}$ or $\frac{1}{5}$ of 150, which is 30.

3 a E **b** C **c** A **d** B **e** D

7 Ratio and proportion

7.1 Direct proportion

Purposeful practice 1

1 a £5 **b** £10 **c** £20 **d** £30 **e** £60 **f** £120
2 a 12 **b** 24 **c** 36 **d** 60 **e** 96 **f** 120

Purposeful practice 2

1 $\frac{1}{2}$ teaspoon **2** $1\frac{1}{2}$ teaspoons **3** 6 teaspoons

4 2 teaspoons **5** $3\frac{1}{2}$ teaspoons **6** $5\frac{1}{2}$ teaspoons

7 11 teaspoons **8** $12\frac{1}{2}$ teaspoons

Purposeful practice 3

1 £5 **2** £15 **3** £20 **4** £25 **5** £30 **6** £35

Problem-solving practice

1 No, 20 is double the amount of people but double the amount of flour is 450 g.
2 a Helen has used the 5 in the question as the price per person, instead of working out the cost of one person by dividing 35 by 5.
b £35 ÷ 5 = £7, 3 × £7 = £21
3 a

Pounds (£)	Euros (€)
9	10
18	**20**
45	**50**
90	**100**

b £72

4 No, 450 ÷ 50 = 9, so the car travels 9 miles per litre.
9 × 6 = 54 miles
5 £45
6 50 g butter, 25 g caster sugar, 175 g flour

7.2 Writing ratios

Purposeful practice 1

1 A 1 : 1, B 1 : 1, C 2 : 1, D 2 : 1, E 1 : 2, F 1 : 2, G 2 : 2 or 1 : 1, H 2 : 2 or 1 : 1
2, 3 Students' own answers showing numbers of coloured tiles given in the question. For example, answer **2a** should show 3 white tiles and 2 grey tiles.

Purposeful practice 2

1 a 2 : 3 **b** 2 : 3 **c** 5 : 3 **d** 2 : 5 **e** 3 : 2 **f** 5 : 3
g 2 : 5 **h** 5 : 2 **i** 3 : 2 **j** 5 : 2
2 a 1 : 2 : 2 **b** 1 : 2 : 3 **c** 1 : 2 : 4 **d** 1 : 1 : 2
e 1 : 1 : 2 **f** 2 : 3 : 4 **g** 1 : 2 : 1 **h** 1 : 2 : 1

Problem-solving practice

1 Tariq has written the numbers the wrong way around: it should be 1 : 2
2 Sophie has halved both 9 and 24 but 9 is not an even number. She should have divided them both by 3 to give 3 : 8
3 Students should shade in 2 sections of the bar black and leave the other 6 sections white.
4 15 ÷ 3 = 5, 20 ÷ 4 = 5 and 30 ÷ 6 = 5. They all have the same answer of 5 so 15 : 20 : 30 simplifies to 3 : 4 : 6
5 12 : 18 and 2 : 3; 30 : 20 and 3 : 2; 28 : 21 and 4 : 3; 9 : 12 and 3 : 4; 25 : 35 and 5 : 7; 56 : 40 and 7 : 5
6 a 14 **b** 5 **c** 49
d 24 **e** 28 **f** 27
7 56 children
8 Yes, as 15 × 12 = 180, so there could be up to 180 students for 15 staff.
9 Yes, as double 4 is 8 and 9 is more than this.
10 a Stuart divided 36 and 60 by 12, and 42 by 6. You must divide all the numbers in the ratio by the same number, so by 6 for this ratio.
b 6 : 7 : 10
c Students should give their own ratio that simplifies to 3 : 7 : 5, such as 6 : 14 : 10

7.3 Using ratios

Purposeful practice 1

1 A, I, K;   B, G, J;   C, F;   D, H
2 a i 7   **ii** 14   **iii** 49   **iv** 175
   b i 2   **ii** 6   **iii** 12   **iv** 40

Purposeful practice 2

1 a 5 cm and 7 cm   **b** 10 cm and 2 cm
   c 9 cm and 3 cm   **d** 8 cm and 4 cm
2 a 2 m and 3 m   **b** 4 m and 6 m
   c 6 m and 9 m   **d** 8 m and 12 m
   e 2 m and 4 m   **f** 4 m and 8 m
   g 2 m and 6 m   **h** 4 m and 12 m

Problem-solving practice

1 Yes, as 4 and 3 multiplied by 4 give 16 and 12 respectively.
2 Students should give three ratios equivalent to 1 : 4, for example, 2 : 8, 3 : 12 and 4 : 16
3 4 : 5, 12 : 15, 32 : 40 and 44 : 55
   6 : 7, 12 : 14, 30 : 35 and 60 : 70
   3 : 5, 12 : 20, 21 : 35 and 27 : 45
4 a Because the missing number would be a decimal, 4.5, for this to work.
   b 2 : 3 and 6 : 9 (× 3), or 2 : 1 and 18 : 9 (× 9)
5 250 g flour and 100 g butter
6 £50
7 a Ava, 30 m   **b** Felix, 15 m   **c** 10 m   **d** 10 m
8 500 ml   **9** 10 kg

7.4 Ratios, proportions and fractions

Purposeful practice 1

1 a i $\frac{1}{3}$ **b i** $\frac{1}{4}$ **c i** $\frac{1}{5}$ **d i** $\frac{2}{5}$
   ii $\frac{2}{3}$ **ii** $\frac{3}{4}$ **ii** $\frac{4}{5}$ **ii** $\frac{3}{5}$

   e i $\frac{1}{3}$ **f i** $\frac{1}{4}$ **g i** $\frac{1}{3}$ **h i** $\frac{1}{4}$
   ii $\frac{2}{3}$ **ii** $\frac{3}{4}$ **ii** $\frac{2}{3}$ **ii** $\frac{3}{4}$

2 a 1 : 2   **b** 1 : 3   **c** 1 : 4   **d** 2 : 3
   e 1 : 2   **f** 1 : 3   **g** 1 : 2   **h** 1 : 3

Purposeful practice 2

1 Adults: 11 am is $\frac{3}{10}$, 2 pm is $\frac{2}{5}$, 5 pm is $\frac{11}{20}$, 8 pm is $\frac{3}{4}$

2 Children: 11 am is $\frac{7}{10}$, 2 pm is $\frac{3}{5}$, 5 pm is $\frac{9}{20}$, 8 pm is $\frac{1}{4}$

3 8 pm. Changing all the proportions to fractions with a denominator of 20, $\frac{3}{4} = \frac{15}{20}$, which is the greatest proportion.

4 11 am. Changing all the proportions to fractions with a denominator of 20, $\frac{7}{10} = \frac{14}{20}$, which is the greatest proportion.

Problem-solving practice

1 No, because the denominator should be the total, 9, so $\frac{4}{9}$
2 a $\frac{2}{5}$ and $\frac{3}{5}$ **b** $\frac{5}{6}$ and $\frac{1}{6}$ **c** $\frac{7}{12}$ and $\frac{5}{12}$ **d** $\frac{2}{9}$ and $\frac{7}{9}$
3 a 1 : 4   **b** 5 : 2   **c** 11 : 4   **d** 9 : 31
4 5 : 2
5 No, as $\frac{2}{10} = \frac{1}{5}$ so the ratios are the same and neither colour is darker.
6 Proportion of food for supermarket A = $\frac{17}{20}$, proportion of food for supermarket B = $\frac{4}{5}$.
   $\frac{4}{5} = \frac{16}{20}$, so supermarket A sells the greater proportion of food.
7 School A: $\frac{180}{250} = \frac{360}{500}$; School B: $\frac{370}{500}$; School C: $\frac{720}{1000} = \frac{360}{500}$
   So School B has the greatest proportion of students within 3 miles.

7.5 Proportions and percentages

Purposeful practice 1

1 a i 70% **b i** 64% **c i** 48% **d i** 40% **e i** 60%
   ii 30%   **ii** 36%   **ii** 52%   **ii** 60%   **ii** 40%
2 a Box 1   **b** Box 4

Purposeful practice 2

1 a 10%   **2 a** 30%   **3 a** 38%   **4 a** 36%
   b 90%   **b** 70%   **b** 62%   **b** 64%
5 a 25%   **6 a** 40%   **7 a** 15%   **8 a** 35%
   b 75%   **b** 60%   **b** 85%   **b** 65%

Problem-solving practice

1 Wes is correct as 3 : 2 = 60 : 40
2 44% and 56%, 11 : 14
   40% and 60%, 2 : 3
   42% and 58%, 21 : 29
   48% and 52%, 12 : 13
3 a 1 : 4   **b** 9 : 11   **c** 3 : 1, 25%   **d** 9 : 16, 64%
4 7 : 13
5 Ethan: 55% red, Melissa: 54% red, so Melissa's shape has the smaller proportion of red.
6 Emily's orange squash is stronger but because 14% of it is squash (not 7%) and only 10% of Jay's is squash.
7 Paper 1: 64% number, Paper 2: 70% number, so Paper 2 has the greater proportion of number questions.
8 a School C as A: $\frac{80}{200}$ = 40%, B: $\frac{9}{30}$ = 30% and C: $\frac{45}{100}$ = 45%
   b School B
9 Seb's ratio is 6 : 200 = 3 : 100; Ajay's ratio is 20 : 500 = 4 : 100.
   So Ajay has the saltier water.

Mixed exercises B

Mixed problem-solving practice B

1 $\frac{3}{4}$ = 75% and 80% − 75% = 5%
2 Students should convert all numbers to the same format, for example, 0.2 = 20%, $\frac{1}{4}$ = 25%, 0.5 = 50%, $\frac{2}{5}$ = 40%
   So the correct order is 0.2, $\frac{1}{4}$, 30%, $\frac{2}{5}$, 0.5
3 17.64   **4** 40 ml
5 Amy, as 10 × 50 = 500, which is much closer to 476.80206 than 4768.0206
6 37.5 litres
7 a 0.45   **b** 48
8 93   **9** 23.05 km   **10** 5220 m²
11 65
12 No, as area of wall = 500 × 300 = 150 000 cm²,
   area of tile = 20 × 20 = 400 cm², 150 000 ÷ 400 = 375,
   375 ÷ 25 = 15,
   15 × £38 = £570 (which is more than what she has).
13 a $\frac{7}{20}$ **b** 5 red, 5 white
14 a 4 : 5   **b** No, as it is $\frac{27}{54}$, which is exactly $\frac{1}{2}$, not over $\frac{1}{2}$
   c Year 10: 25%, Year 11: 30%, so difference = 5%

8 Lines and angles

8.1 Measuring and drawing angles

Purposeful practice 1

1 a 20°   **b** 100°   **c** 160°
2 a 80°   **b** 60°   **c** 40°
3 a 140°   **b** 130°   **c** 110°

Purposeful practice 2

1 a i Acute   **b i** Acute   **c i** Obtuse
   ii 60°   **ii** 80°   **ii** 140°
   d i Obtuse   **e i** Reflex   **f i** Reflex
   ii 100°   **ii** 260°   **ii** 320°
2 a i Acute
   ii Students' own drawing of an angle measuring 20°
   b i Acute
   ii Students' own drawing of an angle measuring 50°
   c i Acute
   ii Students' own drawing of an angle measuring 70°
   d i Obtuse
   ii Students' own drawing of an angle measuring 160°
   e i Obtuse
   ii Students' own drawing of an angle measuring 130°

f i Obtuse

ii Students' own drawing of an angle measuring 110°

g i Reflex

ii Students' own drawing of an angle measuring 200°

h i Reflex

ii Students' own drawing of an angle measuring 230°

i i Reflex

ii Students' own drawing of an angle measuring 250°

Problem-solving practice

1 a Students' own drawing of a right angle, labelled 90°

b Students' own drawing of an acute angle (less than 90°) labelled with the correct measurement.

c Students' own drawing of an obtuse angle (between 90° and 180°) labelled with the correct measurement.

d Students' own drawing of a reflex angle (more than 180°) labelled with the correct measurement.

2 Eric has used the outside scale instead of the inside scale. The angle is acute, not obtuse. It should be 30°.

3 a 72 + 281 = 353, but it should be 360, so Ben is 7° off in total and his answer cannot be correct.

b $a = 75°$ and $b = 285°$

4 60°

5 Green is 115°, red is 110°, yellow 95° and blue 40°. Green is the largest angle, therefore Vicki shaded more green than any other colour.

8.2 Lines, angles and triangles

Purposeful practice 1

1 Angle at D: ∠FDE or ∠EDF, angle at E: ∠DEF or ∠FED, angle at F: ∠DFE or ∠EFD

2 a angle PQR, ∠PQR, PQ̂R, angle RQP, RQ̂P, ∠RQP

b They have 'Q' in the middle.

Purposeful practice 2

1 a i 48°, 48°, 84° **ii** Isosceles

b i 60°, 60°, 60° **ii** Equilateral

c i 71°, 71°, 38° **ii** Isosceles

2 a i 37°, 53°, 90° **ii** Right-angled scalene

b i 45°, 45°, 90° **ii** Right-angled isosceles

c i 30°, 56°, 94° **ii** Scalene

Problem-solving practice

1 a C **b** A **c** B

2 ∠RQP

3 ∠BCA is clearly smaller than ∠CAB, so these numbers cannot be right.

He should have ∠ABC = 70°, ∠BCA = 30° and ∠CAB = 80°

4 a Isosceles **b** Scalene **c** Equilateral

5 A and D, as these have two sides the same length

6 Yes, as all of the sides are the same and the angles are all 60°

8.3 Drawing triangles accurately

Purposeful practice 1

Throughout this exercise, students should draw accurate drawings of each sketch, with the measurements shown in the question.

Purposeful practice 2

1 C **2** B

3 Throughout this question students should draw accurate drawings of each triangle from **Q1** and **Q2**, with measurements equal to those shown in each question.

Problem-solving practice

1 a i B **ii** D **iii** A **iv** C

b Students should draw accurate drawings of each triangle, using the measurements given in the question.

2 The angle is correct but XZ = 10.2 cm

3 No, the height is only 4 cm

4 Students' diagrams should be drawn to scale using the measurements shown. This diagram is not drawn to scale.

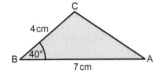

5 Students' diagrams should be drawn to scale using the measurements shown. This diagram is not drawn to scale.

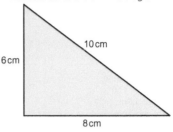

6 A and D

8.4 Calculating angles

Purposeful practice 1

1 $a = 90°$, $b = 80°$, $c = 30°$, $d = 150°$, $e = 120°$, $f = 95°$

2 $a = 90°$, $b = 60°$, $c = 45°$, $d = 36°$, $e = 30°$

Purposeful practice 2

1 $a = 80°$, $b = 80°$, $c = 30°$

2 $a = 270°$, $b = 180°$, $c = 260°$, $d = 240°$, $e = 210°$, $f = 200°$

3 $a = 90°$, $b = 72°$, $c = 60°$

Problem-solving practice

1 a If angle a is 50° then $4 \times 50° = 200°$, but the angles on a straight line only add up to 180°.

b $a = 30°$

2 140° + 120° + 90° = 350°, but the angles around a point add up to 360°. Angle $x = 100°$

3 Angle a is bigger because $a = 180° \div 5 = 36°$ and $b = (180° - 145°) = 35°$

4 150° and 210°

5 C and E; B, D and G; A, F and H

8.5 Angles in a triangle

Purposeful practice 1

1 $a = 40°$, $b = 30°$, $c = 65°$, $d = 35°$, $e = 45°$, $f = 38°$, $g = 28°$, $h = 18°$

Purposeful practice 2

1 $a = 30°$, $b = 40°$, $c = 70°$

2 $a = 30°$, $b = 20°$, $c = 60°$

3 $a = 20°$, $b = 10°$, $c = 30°$

4 $d = 70°$, $e = 40°$, $f = 62°$, $g = 56°$, $h = 52°$, $i = 76°$

5 $j = k = 55°$, $l = m = 59°$, $n = p = 64°$

Problem-solving practice

1 Because 42 + 75 + 73 = 190 and angles in a triangle add up to 180°

2 a $a = 65°$ **b** $b = 36°$

3 a They have both identified the two equal angles incorrectly. James has said angles a and 70° are equal and Steph has said angles a and b are equal, but it is angle b and 70° that are equal.

b $a = 40°$ and $b = 70°$

4 No, as the angles in an equilateral triangle are all equal, 180 ÷ 3 = 60, so they are all 60°

5 Angle BAC = 75° and angle ACB = 25°

6 $a = 50°$, $b = 60°$, $c = 70°$

8.6 Quadrilaterals

Purposeful practice

1 a Kite, arrowhead

b Isosceles trapezium

c Square, rectangle, parallelogram, rhombus

2 a Rectangle, parallelogram, kite, arrowhead

b Square, rhombus

c Square, rectangle, parallelogram, isosceles trapezium, rhombus

d Square, rhombus, kite, arrowhead

3 a Square, rectangle

b Square, rectangle

c Parallelogram, rhombus, isosceles trapezium

d Kite, arrowhead

e Square, rectangle, kite, rhombus, parallelogram, arrowhead

4 a Two pairs of equal sides, equal sides opposite each other, two pairs of equal angles, equal angles diagonally opposite each other.

b Two pairs of parallel sides, four equal sides, two pairs of equal angles, equal angles opposite each other

Problem-solving practice

1

	Only one pair of equal angles	Two pairs of angles are equal	All four angles are equal
Sides next to each other are equal	Kite Arrowhead		
Only one pair of opposite sides are parallel		Isosceles trapezium	
Opposite sides are equal and parallel		Parallelogram	Rectangle
All four sides are equal		Rhombus	Square

2 a Rhombus **b** Square **c** Isosceles trapezium

3 A Square, B Parallelogram, C Kite, D Rhombus, E Isosceles trapezium

4 $a = 145°$, $b = 35°$, $c = 7$ cm, $d = 7$ cm, $e = 7$ cm, $f = 90°$, $g = 90°$, $h = 90°$, $j = 90°$, $k = 5$ cm, $l = 9$ cm

9 Sequences and graphs

9.1 Sequences

Purposeful practice 1

1 a 3, 5, 7, 9 **b** 3, 6, 12, 24 **c** 9, 7, 5, 3
   d 24, 12, 6, 3 **e** 20, 23, 26, 29 **f** 20, 17, 14, 11
   g 1, 3, 9, 27 **h** 27, 9, 3, 1

2 a Ascending **b** Ascending **c** Descending
   d Descending **e** Ascending **f** Descending
   g Ascending **h** Descending

3 a 14, 17; rule is '+ 3' **b** 3, 0; rule is '− 3'
   c 18, 23; rule is '+ 5' **d** 12, 7; rule is '− 5'
   e 994, 992; rule is '− 2' **f** 532, 534; rule is '+ 2'
   g 250, 125; rule is '÷ 2' **h** 8, 16; rule is '× 2'
   i 40, 80; rule is '× 2' **j** 80, 160; rule is '× 2'
   k 100, 50; rule is '÷ 2' **l** 9970, 9960; rule is '− 10'
   m 10, 1; rule is '÷ 10' **n** 2000, 20 000; rule is '× 10'
   o 2030, 2040; rule is '+ 10'

Purposeful practice 2

1 a 6, 5, 4, 3 **b** 6, 4, 2, 0 **c** 6, 3, 0, −3
   d 6, 0, −6, −12 **e** −5, 0, 5, 10 **f** −5, −1, 3, 7
   g −5, −3, −1, 1 **h** −5, −4, −3, −2

2 a 3, 1, −1, −3 **b** 2, 0, −2, −4 **c** 1, −1, −3, −5
   d −1, −3, −5, −7 **e** −2, −4, −6, −8 **f** −2, −5, −8, −11
   g −2, −7, −12, −17

3 a 7, $7\frac{1}{2}$, 8, $8\frac{1}{2}$ **b** 7, 7.2, 7.4, 7.6 **c** 7, 6.7, 6.4, 6.1
   d 7, $6\frac{1}{2}$, 6, $5\frac{1}{2}$ **e** 20, 20.1, 20.2, 20.3
   f 20, 2, 0.2, 0.02 **g** 8.4, 6.4, 4.4, 2.4 **h** 8.4, 4.2, 2.1, 1.05

Problem-solving practice

1 No, as 1 + 4 = 5 but 5 + 4 ≠ 25, etc. The term-to-term rule is '× 5'.

2 a 14 and 20 **b** 90 and 70 **c** 22 and 27
   d 12 and 26 **e** −7 and −11 **f** 8.6 and 8.0

3 No; students should give a suitable explanation. For example, 36 is an even number and the numbers in the sequence are odd numbers.

4 Student C is correct, as the term-to-term rule for the sequence is '−5' and 3 − 5 = −2 and −2 − 5 = −7

5 7

6 4.2, 4.5, 4.8, 5.1, 5.4 or 4.5, 4.7, 4.9, 5.1, 5.3

7 a 19 or 100 **b** + 9 or × 10 **c** 19, 28, 37 or 100, 1000, 10 000

8 Students should write a first term and a term-to-term rule for a descending sequence that includes the term 8.3, for example, first term 8.6 and term-to-term rule '−0.3'

9 26, 33, 40, 47, 54 and 50, 46, 42, 38, 34

9.2 Pattern sequences

Purposeful practice 1

2 a 1 **b** 1, 5, 9 **c** + 4
   d There is one dot in the first pattern. 4 dots are added each time.

3 a 1 **b** 1, 5, 9 **c** + 4
   d There is one square in the first pattern. 4 squares are added each time.

4 a 3 **b** 3, 5, 7 **c** + 2
   d There 3 lines in the first pattern. 2 lines are added each time.

5 a 5 **b** 5, 9, 13 **c** + 4
   d There 5 lines in the first pattern. 4 lines are added each time.

Purposeful practice 2

1 a 2 × 3 **b** 2 × 4 **c** 2 × 10
2 a 3 × 3 **b** 3 × 4 **c** 3 × 10
3 a 4 × 3 **b** 5 × 4 **c** 11 × 10
4 a 6 × 3 **b** 8 × 4 **c** 20 × 10

Problem-solving practice

1 A 15, B 17, C 11, D 16

2 31

3 No, as all of the patterns in the sequence use an odd number of matchsticks and 14 is even

4 No, as the rectangles in the sequence are all 4 × ☐

5 a 7 **b** 1

6 B and C **7** 2

9.3 Coordinates and midpoints

Purposeful practice 1

1 a 2, 3, 4, 5, 6, 7
   b y-values sequence first term 2, term-to-term rule '+ 1'
   c Axes with (0, 2), (1, 3), (2, 4), (3, 5), (4, 6) and (5, 7) plotted

2 a −2, −1, 0, 1, 2, 3
   b y-values sequence first term −2, term-to-term rule '+ 1'
   c Axes with (0, −2), (1, −1), (2, 0), (3, 1), (4, 2) and (5, 3) plotted

Purposeful practice 2

1

Line segment	Beginning point	Endpoint	Midpoint
AB	(2, 8)	(2, 2)	(2, 5)
CD	(5, 3)	(5, −3)	(5, 0)
EF	(−4, 8)	(−4, 0)	(−4, 4)
GH	(−7, 3)	(−7, −1)	(−7, 1)

2

Line segment	Beginning point	Endpoint	Midpoint
JK	(2, 6)	(8, 6)	(5, 6)
LM	(−8, 2)	(−2, 2)	(−5, 2)
NP	(1, −3)	(7, −3)	(4, −3)
QR	(1, 1)	(3, 3)	(2, 2)
ST	(3, 0)	(7, 2)	(5, 1)
UV	(−4, 9)	(−2, 3)	(−3, 6)

Problem-solving practice

1 a The line on the graph is not a straight line.
   b 2 and 3. They should be 3 and 4.

c

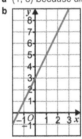

d Yes, because when you add 5 to the x-coordinate it is equal to the y-coordinate, i.e. $5 + 5 = 10$

2 (6, 5)

3 a (0, 0)   **b** (−4, 4)   **c** (−2, 1)

4 a (3, 3)   **b** (2, 2)   **c** (4, 4)   **d** (3, 5)

9.4 Extending sequences

Purposeful practice 1

1 a Add 3; arithmetic   **b** Add 4; arithmetic
  c Subtract 2; arithmetic   **d** Add 3; arithmetic
  e Add 2; arithmetic   **f** Add 1; arithmetic
  g Multiply by 2; not arithmetic **h** Multiply by 3; not arithmetic
  i Add 2; arithmetic   **j** Divide by 10; not arithmetic
  k Divide by 2; not arithmetic **l** Subtract 30; arithmetic

2 a 3, 6, 12, 24; not arithmetic **b** 3, 7, 15, 31; not arithmetic
  c 3, 5, 9, 17; not arithmetic **d** 3, 8, 18, 38; not arithmetic
  e 3, 4, 6, 10; not arithmetic

Purposeful practice 2

1 b 19

2 a

Pattern Number	1	2	3	4
Sequence	1	4	7	10

  b 1st pattern 1
    2nd pattern $1 + 1 \times 3 = 4$
    3rd pattern $1 + 2 \times 3 = 7$
    4th pattern $1 + 3 \times 3 = 10$
    10th pattern $1 + 9 \times 3 = 28$

3 a

Pattern Number	1	2	3	4
Sequence	2	3	4	5

  b 1st pattern 2
    2nd pattern $2 + 1 \times 1 = 3$
    3rd pattern $2 + 2 \times 1 = 4$
    4th pattern $2 + 3 \times 1 = 5$
    10th pattern $2 + 9 \times 1 = 11$

4 a

Pattern Number	1	2	3	4
Sequence	1	5	9	13

  b 1st pattern 1
    2nd pattern $1 + 1 \times 4 = 5$
    3rd pattern $1 + 2 \times 4 = 9$
    4th pattern $1 + 3 \times 4 = 13$
    10th pattern $1 + 9 \times 4 = 37$

5 a

Pattern Number	1	2	3	4
Sequence	4	5	6	7

  b 1st pattern 4
    2nd pattern $4 + 1 \times 1 = 5$
    3rd pattern $4 + 2 \times 1 = 6$
    4th pattern $4 + 3 \times 1 = 7$
    10th pattern $4 + 9 \times 1 = 13$

Problem-solving practice

1 Yes, as sequence does not go up in equal steps; it increases by 2, then 4, then 8, etc.

2 No, as the numbers in the sequence always have 3 in the ones column (3, 13, 23, 33, 43, etc.) but 65 has a 5 in the ones column.

3 8

4 a 16, 23, 30 **b** 94, 88, 82 **c** 16, 11, 6 **d** 4.7, 4.4, 4.1

5 A 30, B 21, C 31, D 37

6 55

9.5 Straight-line graphs

Purposeful practice 1

1 A: $y = 5$, B: $y = -5$, C: $x = -5$, D: $x = 5$, E: $x = 1$, F: $y = 1$, G: $y = -3$, H: $x = -3$

2 a x-axis   **b** y-axis

Purposeful practice 2

1 a

x	−5	−4	−3	−2	−1	0	1	2	3	4	5
y	−5	−4	−3	−2	−1	0	1	2	3	4	5

b

x	−5	−4	−3	−2	−1	0	1	2	3	4	5
y	5	4	3	2	1	0	−1	−2	−3	−4	−5

c Graphs of $y = x$ and $y = -x$

2 a

x	0	1	2	3	4
y	1	2	3	4	5

b

x	0	1	2	3	4
y	0	2	4	6	8

c

x	0	1	2	3	4
y	1	3	5	7	9

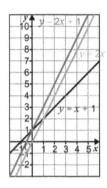

Problem-solving practice

1 a C   **b** G   **c** B   **d** F
  e D   **f** H   **g** A   **h** E

2 (5, 3), (5, 5), (5, 0) and (5, −5) because the x-coordinate is 5 for each of these coordinates.

3 No, Sonia has drawn the correct graphs but has got the labels the wrong way round.

4 a 0, 3, 6, 9, 12, 15   **b** 3
  c Yes, as $8 \times 3 = 24$

5 a (1, 8) because all of the other points are on a straight line.
  b

9.6 Position-to-term rules

Purposeful practice 1

1 2, 4, 6, 8, 10   **2** 4, 8, 12, 16, 20
3 7, 14, 21, 28, 35   **4** 10, 20, 30, 40, 50

Purposeful practice 2

1 a i 4, 8, 12, 16, 20 **ii** 4   **b i** 5, 9, 13, 17, 21 **ii** 4
  c i 3, 7, 11, 15, 19 **ii** 4   **d i** 7, 11, 15, 19, 23 **ii** 4
2 a i 3, 6, 9, 12, 15 **ii** 3   **b i** 5, 8, 11, 14, 17 **ii** 3
  c i 1, 4, 7, 10, 13 **ii** 3   **d i** 2, 5, 8, 11, 14 **ii** 3
3 a i 6, 12, 18, 24, 30 **ii** 6   **b i** 7, 13, 19, 25, 31 **ii** 6
  c i 11, 17, 23, 29, 35 **ii** 6   **d i** 5, 11, 17, 23, 29 **ii** 6

Purposeful practice 3

1 a i 2, 4, 6, 8, 10   **ii** multiples of 2
  b i 3, 5, 7, 9, 11   **ii** multiples of 2, plus 1
  c i 5, 7, 9, 11, 13   **ii** multiples of 2, plus 3
  d i −1, 1, 3, 5, 7   **ii** multiples of 2, subtract 3
  e i 1, 3, 5, 7, 9   **ii** multiples of 2, subtract 1
2 a i 5, 10, 15, 20, 25   **ii** multiples of 5
  b i 6, 11, 16, 21, 26   **ii** multiples of 5, plus 1

c i 7, 12, 17, 22, 27   **ii** multiples of 5, plus 2
d i 3, 8, 13, 18, 23   **ii** multiples of 5, subtract 2
e i 4, 9, 14, 19, 24   **ii** multiples of 5, subtract 1

Problem-solving practice

1 No, as 13 and 16 are not the 4th and 5th multiple of 3. They should be 12 and 15.
2 D   **3** 5
4 A and K, B and G, C and L, D and H, E and J, F and I
5 47
6 Students' own answers involving a substitution into the sequence. For example, the second term of the sequence is 17, which is odd.
7 No, as the numbers in the sequence are all odd numbers and 30 is even.
8 4
9 a $7n$ **b** $5n - 2$ **c** $5n + 6$
10 D
11 A because when $n = 1$, the first term is $2(1) + 3 = 5$, and this sequence would go up in increments of 2.

10 Transformations

10.1 Congruency and enlargements

Purposeful practice 1
1 C, E, G   **2** A, C and D

Purposeful practice 2
1
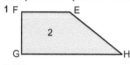
2 EH
3
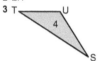

Purposeful practice 3
1 3   **2** 4   **3** $1\frac{1}{2}$

Problem-solving practice
1 a No, as the two shapes aren't exactly the same shape and size.
  b Yes, as the two shapes are exactly the same shape and size.
2 90 cm
3 B is an enlargement of scale factor 6 and E is an enlargement of scale factor 2
4 No, as he hasn't drawn the sides long enough. The height of the triangle should be 4 squares, not 3, and the base should be 6 squares, not 5.
5 If you multiply the length of each of the sides of shape A by 3, they all equal the corresponding sides on shape B. Alternatively, if you divide each of the lengths of shape B by the corresponding lengths on shape A, the answers are all 3.

10.2 Symmetry

Purposeful practice 1
1
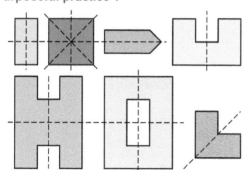

Purposeful practice 2
1 a 0   **b** 1   **2 a** 1   **b** 1
3 a 3   **b** 3   **4 a** 0   **b** 1

Purposeful practice 3
1 9 cm   **2** 75°   **3** 10 cm   **4** 70°

Problem-solving practice
1 a True, as all the sides are different lengths.
  b False, as only two sides are equal so there is only one line of symmetry.
  c True, as all sides are equal.
  d True, as all four sides are equal, but only opposite angles are equal (not all four equal like a square).
  e False, as opposite sides are equal (not all four equal like a square) so there are only two lines of symmetry.
2 a No, as one part of the shape does not exactly fold on to the other part of the shape in all cases (the lines through the midpoints of the sides of the rhombus, and the horizontal on the kite are wrong).
  b No, as a rhombus has rotational symmetry order 2 and a kite doesn't have rotational symmetry (order 1).
3 Examples of answers:
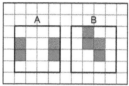

4 a Student's own answers, for example, any three triangles shaded where exactly two of them are adjacent
  b Students' own answers, for example, all but two opposite triangles shaded
  c Students' own answers, for example, two opposite triangles shaded
  d Student's own answers, for example, three triangles shaded with blanks between each
5 Students' own answers, for example, an isosceles triangle or a kite

10.3 Reflection

Purposeful practice 1
1
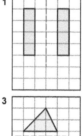
2
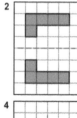
3
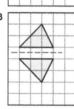
4
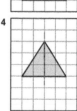

Purposeful practice 2
1 a G   **b** C   **c** H   **d** I   **e** F   **f** I
2
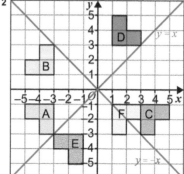

Problem-solving practice

1 C, as it has been reflected in the correct position, 1 square from the mirror line. A hasn't been reflected, it's just moved right 4 squares, and B has been reflected but not in the correct position (as the reflection is touching the mirror line).

2 No, Maylia has rotated the shape not reflected it. The point (2, 5) on triangle A reflects to (5, 2) and point (−3, 2) reflects to (2, −3).

3 **a** $x = -1$ **b** $x = 0$ or the y-axis   **c** $x = -1$
d $y = 1$ **e** $y = x$

4 **a**

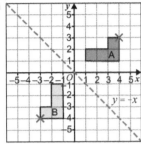

b (4, 3)   **c** (−3, −4)
d The numbers have become negative and the digits have swapped, so x has become $-y$ and vice versa.
e Yes; the same is true for all other points on the shapes. For example, the corner at (4, 1) reflects to (−1, −4) and so on.

10.4 Rotation

Purposeful practice 1

1 A: 90° anticlockwise; B: 90° clockwise; C: 180°; D: 90° anticlockwise; E: 180°; F: 180°

2 **a**

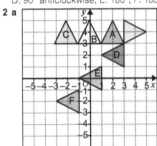

b A (1, 3), (3, 3), (2, 5)
B (−1, 3), (1, 3), (0, 5)
C (−3, 3), (−1, 3), (−2, 5)
D (3, 3), (3, 1), (1, 2)
E (1, 1), (1, −1), (−1, 0)
F (−1, −1), (−1, −3), (−3, −2)

Purposeful practice 2

1 90° clockwise about (2, 1)
2 90° anticlockwise about (2, 1)
3 90° anticlockwise about (3, −2)
4 90° clockwise about (3, −2)
5 90° anticlockwise about (−2, −3)

Problem-solving practice

1 **a** The rotation of shape A is the correct way around but is in the wrong position. Shape B has been reflected, not rotated.
b

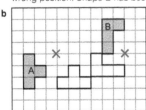

2 The rotation is 180° but the centre of rotation (1, 2) rotates shape A to (−1, 2), (−1, −1), (−3, −1). The centre of rotation is (1, 1).

3 **a** **i** A onto E   **ii** B onto C   **iii** C onto G   **iv** F onto G
v B onto D   **vi** G onto D
b E onto F is a 90° rotation anticlockwise about (2, −4)

10.5 Translations and combined transformations

Purposeful practice 1

1 **a** 2 squares up   **b** 3 squares right
c 5 squares down   **d** 6 squares left
e 3 squares right, 2 squares up
f 3 squares right, 5 squares down
g 6 squares left, 2 squares up
h 5 squares left, 7 squares down

2

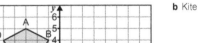
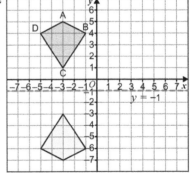

Purposeful practice 2

1 D   2 E   3 B   4 C   5 F   6 A

Problem-solving practice

1 A translation doesn't go by the squares in between the shapes; if you pick a corner on rectangle A and the corresponding corner on the translated rectangle, it is 6 squares right and 3 squares up.

2 No, as triangle Q is facing the wrong way and triangle R is a different-sized triangle.

3 **a** 2 squares right and 3 squares down
b 2 squares left and 3 squares up
c The two answers are the same numbers but opposite directions right/left and down/up. This works for all translations. Students should draw two different examples to demonstrate this.

4 **b** G onto F   **c** E onto D   **d** F onto E   **e** D onto C
f C onto H   **g** A onto B

Mixed exercises C

Mixed problem-solving practice C

1 **a** (2, 3)   **b** (−2, 2)   **c** (−1, −1)   **d** Acute angle
e i 2   **ii** (4, −3) and (−4, −5)
2 Parallelogram
3 **a** and **c**   **b** Kite

4 **a** Reflection in the line $y = -1$
b Rotation 90° anticlockwise about (0, 0)
5 **a** $x = 41°$, as $180 - 56 = 124$ and $180 - 124 - 15 = 41$
b $x = 125°$, as $180 - 90 - 35 = 55$ and $180 - 55 = 125$
c $x = 78°$, as $360 - 290 = 70$, $180 - 148 = 32$ and $180 - 70 - 32 = 78$

6 a $x = 40°$. The angles in the equilateral triangle are 60° each as they are all equal. The base angles in the isosceles triangles are equal, so they are 70° each because the 160° angle, an angle in the equilateral triangle and two base angles in the isosceles triangle make a full turn of 360°. The angles in a triangle total 180°.

b The six sides of the perimeter are all the same length, so divide 84 by 6 (so $y = 14\,cm$).

7 No. Students may draw the diagram to demonstrate that triangles E and C are in different positions. D should have been reflected in the x-axis, not the y-axis, for this to have been true.

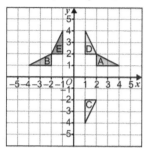

8 a

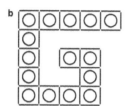

c

Pattern number	1	2	3	4	5	6	7	8	9	10
Number of lines	4	7	10	13	16	19	22	25	28	31

d Students' own explanation, for example, Hamish could keep adding on 3 until he gets to the 30th pattern, or he could multiply 30 by 3 and then add on 1.

e 91   **f** 30   **g** 8

h The maximum sized spiral that fits across the wallpaper is pattern 44. So number of lines is $44 \times 3 + 1 = 133$.

Index